MW00610293

Scandinavian from Scratch

Gravlax and Chive Potato Salad Smørrebrød, page 214

Scandinavian from Scratch

A Love Letter to the Baking of Denmark, Norway, and Sweden

Nichole Accettola
with Malena Watrous

Photographs By Anders Schønnemann

TEN SPEED PRESS
California | New York

CONTENTS

THE COOKIE TIN

SIMPLE CAKES AND CELEBRATION DESSERTS

LET'S FIKA!

RISE AND SHINE

RYE BREAD AND SMØRREBRØD

WINTER THERAPY

Cardamom Morning Buns, page 141

For Mom, who would have proudly laminated the pages of this book and used them as placemats. I miss you.

Summer Strawberry Tart with Custard and Chocolate, page 91

Photograph: Alanna Hale

A BAKING LOVE LETTER

I first set foot in Copenhagen at age eighteen, the summer after graduating from high school. Back in Ohio, I'd become close friends with Malene, a Danish exchange student who spent a year at my school, and so I left home to spend that summer with her family. I instantly fell in love with the Danish way of life. We went everywhere by bike. Until then, growing up in rural, hilly Ohio, I had barely biked anywhere and became enamored of this new mode of transportation, using my own legs to get me wherever I needed to go! Because Scandinavia is so far north, the sun practically never sets in summer, and so birds chirp through the night, which I found disorienting and delightful. And that summer I also became smitten with the baked goods there: breads, danishes, cookies, cakes—all of it!

Rather than reserving a sweet treat for after dinner, Danes seize every chance to enjoy fresh baked goods during the day. Many days started with a thick slice of Kringle (page 155) or a Grovbirkes (page 152), and there was almost always an afternoon coffee break with a square of Coconut Dream Cake (page 71), a Cinnamon Knot (page 113), or a Tebirkes (page 149), the almond-filled pastry that is to Denmark what the pain au chocolat is to France. Most of the foods I ate that first summer in Denmark weren't entirely unfamiliar. But somehow they tasted new. I still remember the first time I popped a tiny Danish strawberry into my mouth. It was candy sweet and ruby red, so soft it required minimal chewing. Scandinavian strawberry season is fairly short but enjoyed to the fullest. All summer long, we feasted on strawberry tarts, ate them tossed onto whipped cream–covered cakes, and heaped them by the spoonful into bowls of Buttermilk "Soup" with Cardamom Rusks (page 103) on top, served in lieu of dinner on the hottest summer nights.

I'd had plenty of strawberries in my life, but never any quite as delicate and perfect as those Danish ones. I'd eaten more than my share of cookies, but never tried crumbling them into a bowl of cold, lightly sweetened buttermilk soup. That first summer in Denmark was a revelation. I fell in love with the way that Danes took pleasure in the season, from leisurely bike rides to outdoor dinners going long into the night to weekend music festivals and bonfires.

↟ ↟ ↟ ↟

I returned to the United States that fall to attend culinary school. Becoming a chef had been my dream ever since my mom and I obsessively watched cooking shows together when I was little. Julia Child was my favorite! After graduating from the Culinary Institute of America, I spent nearly ten years working in fine dining in Boston. I never regretted my decision to become a chef. But after a decade, the long hours took a toll, and I craved a more balanced way of life. I'd stayed close with Malene, and she'd introduced me to a Danish guy with whom I'd had a long-distance romance for several years. While I'd visited Joachim often (and vice versa), we wanted to be able to spend more time together, and I also felt drawn to life in Scandinavia, so I thought, *Why not move to Denmark and start a new chapter, aiming for a better work/life balance?* Three weeks after arriving in Copenhagen, we somewhat impulsively married at city hall. But that quick decision turned out to be a great one, as we have been married for over twenty years now and have three kids, all born in Denmark.

As a chef, I'd always dreamed of getting culinary experience in Europe. But at the time, Scandinavia was still far from becoming the culinary destination it is now. I worked at a variety of jobs while we lived there, all in some way related to food and cooking. I was head chef at a preschool, where we prepared made-from-scratch organic meals four times a day (!) for 240 kids. And I worked for a city-run organization, where I led hands-on cooking classes with public school cooks (many of whom were untrained refugees from Afghanistan, Turkey, Somalia, and Bosnia), teaching them culinary skills, including how to incorporate seasonality and be more organized in the kitchen. Naturally, my course recipe lists always included the ubiquitous rye bread that has pride of place at the Danish table. Living in Denmark brought the life balance I sought. I didn't have to give up my career, I was able to cook something other than the Italian/French food I'd previously specialized in, and I learned a new language, and before long this foreign and beloved culture came to feel like my own.

I watched Copenhagen (and the Nordic region) assume an exciting new importance on the global culinary scene after René Redzepi founded Noma in the city in 2003, a restaurant that would go on to receive three Michelin stars and be named best in the world by *Restaurant* magazine. (As of this writing it's set to close.) An influx of chefs and bakers from around the globe came to work at Noma, and many stuck around to open up places of their own, a trickle-down gastronomy that benefited the casual restaurant scene, too. To my immense delight, the number of quality bakeries in the city boomed. I love nothing more than a flaky pastry, and as the bakeries in Copenhagen got better and better, one of my favorite things to do was to go with a friend on a "pastry crawl." This entails waking up extra early to bike around the city, sampling and comparing baked goods from one place to the next, and always

Seeded Savory Pastries, page 152
Poppy Seed and Almond Pastries, page 149

concludes with a feeling of deep satisfaction tinged with a hint of nausea from overindulging.

Copenhagen came to feel like a second home. But after sixteen years of living abroad and only returning to the US for vacation, Joachim and I wanted our three kids to get greater exposure to my culture. So, seven years ago, our family left on what was supposed to be a six-month trip to San Francisco. But those first six months flew by, and we realized that we weren't ready to leave. While I was blown away by the Bay Area's abundant produce and vibrant food scene, we did miss the Scandinavian-style rye bread that had been the staple of our diet back in Denmark, a sentiment shared by many of the Scandinavian expats with whom our paths crossed. So, I set to work trying to develop my *own* recipe for sprouted rye bread as a cure for homesickness. I spent a year on that recipe. Once I felt like I'd perfected it, I started selling it by the loaf, along with smørrebrød (see page 200), the open-faced sandwiches that are a specialty in Denmark, at a stand that I ran with my daughter's help at the Ferry Building farmers' market. It was here that the idea for Kantine, our Scandinavian-inspired venture, was born. A year later, Kantine, our daytime restaurant and bakery, opened its doors.

At Kantine, our motto, scrawled in chalk on a sandwich board sign in front of the restaurant, is "Scandinavian from Scratch." Everything that can be made from scratch is, from the Sprouted Rye Bread (page 198), which also goes into our Rye and Oat Granola (page 183), to our whey-simmered savory and sweet porridges, freshly cultured yogurt, cured trout, bacon, and, of course, the ever-popular Cardamom Morning Buns (page 141), Cinnamon Knots, and Tebirkes. In Scandinavia, people try hard not to waste, and we mimic that sentiment in our kitchen. When almond filling oozes out of the edges of the tebirkes and caramelizes into brittle on the baking tray, we collect the pieces to add to the dough for our Rye Chocolate Chunk Cookies (page 60).

Even though California's seasons are far less extreme than those of Scandinavia, there are still shifts in produce throughout the year. Come spring, we slice up the luscious strawberries to arrange on top of strawberry tarts, just like the ones I ate in Denmark that first summer. In December, we sell a popular assortment of Scandinavian holiday cookies and a Swedish Cardamom Wreath (page 123) that people can buy baked or frozen raw to thaw, proof, and bake at home, filling their own kitchens with that heavenly scent of spices, sugar, and butter. After the December holidays, we celebrate "semla season," serving tender, sweet buns filled with almond paste and whipped cream, which our customers can't seem to get enough of (you'll find the recipe on page 127).

Danish smørrebrød are intended to be as pleasing to the eye as they are to the mouth. I love the care that goes into making each open-faced sandwich, from buttering the bread from crust to crust to layering toppings in a way that shows off the ingredients. Sometimes our open-faced sandwiches are classic combinations, like the Egg and Shrimp Smørrebrød (page 207), but we often create modern takes on a theme, as in the case of the Roasted Cauliflower, Tarragon Cream, and Almond Smørrebrød (page 204). It brings me pleasure to contemplate what flavors and textures will complement each other on these sandwiches, adorning them with pretty garnishes like thinly sliced radishes or fresh herbs.

Because Scandinavian weather fluctuates so much from one season to the next, the region's cooking is deeply influenced by seasonality and the weather. With that comes a great appreciation for nature and a fondness for foraging for ingredients. Foraging might sound a little "out there," or inaccessible to the average home cook (or person living in an urban area), but it doesn't have to be. Foraging can mean picking a few handfuls of wild blackberries growing in a corner of a park. In the Bay Area and in Scandinavia, I have been able to forage all kinds of edible flowers, like wild radish, chamomile, and sorrel, as well as greens of wild onions, stinging nettle, and nasturtium. There's something magical about finding food for free in the wild and realizing that even cities still have patches of wildness. Using what's right in front of me instead of purchasing something for a recipe always makes me feel resourceful, and often the dish tastes more special than one made with standard grocery store ingredients.

I love cooking from the bottom up, being able to play an active role in creating the final result just the way I want it, as I deem the most delicious and delectable. Knowing what my foods are made out of makes me feel like I'm in control of what I put in my body. When I write that, it's not at all from a what's "healthy" and what's "not healthy" perspective. I enjoy eating food, and a fair amount of it isn't "health food," but I love it just the same. I really want to eat a cake that is made with eggs, butter, vanilla, flour, and sugar. I really don't want to eat a cake that is made from a box when I don't know what half of the ingredients are, and it's frankly not worth it.

Thankfully, a lot of Scandinavian baking is relatively simple, using ingredients that most people have already. The Scandinavian emphasis on simplicity and organic forms means that novice bakers can readily learn how to create the cookies, pastries, breads, and other recipes found in these pages, while slightly more advanced bakers will appreciate learning how to fill buns, knot dough, and assemble meringue cakes and tarts.

Rye Crispbread, page 175

Kantine filled a hole in the culinary landscape of San Francisco, where there were lots of great bakeries but none featuring the baked goods representative of the vast Scandinavian baking tradition. In a way, the vastness of that tradition made for a challenge when it came time to choose exactly which cookies, pastries, and cakes to serve. I faced that same challenge when deciding what baking recipes to include in this cookbook.

Every recipe in these pages is either a Scandinavian classic, like St. Lucia Day Saffron Buns (page 243) or Cinnamon Knots, or a Scandinavian-inspired recipe with my own twist. Each chapter begins with the simplest recipes before moving to more complex ones, so keep that in mind if you're just starting out as a baker. But even the more difficult recipes, like the ones using Danish Dough (page 135), aren't really that hard if you follow the steps and allow ample time.

In baking, as in all things, try to set perfectionism aside. Any baked good made from scratch and with love is bound to taste better than anything you can buy, and if it's not perfect, no one will mind! Also, it gives you the opportunity to try again at some point. Becoming a better baker is totally doable with the desire to improve and some practice.

Assembling this cookbook made me reflect upon the role that baked goods play in our lives. We tend to bake for others as much as for ourselves, often for celebrations like birthdays and holidays. When we bake on an ordinary day, the very fact of having a special baked good makes it much less so. We bake (and enjoy baked goods) for comfort. It can often feel like a meditative act, a way of being present in the moment and enjoying the sensations it yields. When we bake together, we delight in sharing in the process as well as the results.

I know that I've forged some of my closest bonds in various kitchens. It feels to me like cooking and baking are a way that you make yourself feel at home no matter where you are. Cooking and baking in a new place help to turn it into a home. And if you bring the recipes and traditions from a place that you've left to your new home, they create a bridge between the two. It's my belief that food that is made from scratch and with care (plus a bit of know-how) will always be worthwhile and heartfelt. That is one of the driving forces behind this cookbook. I am excited to share this Scandinavian culinary love letter with you, so that you can make some of my favorite things in your own kitchen completely from scratch.

SCANDINAVIAN BAKING: AN OVERVIEW

In the United States, people often use the terms *Scandinavian* and *Nordic* interchangeably, so there can be confusion about what the difference (if any) might be. Scandinavia is made up of Norway, Sweden, and Denmark, three countries that share (Scandinavian) linguistic roots and a Viking history. The Nordic region is broader, including those three countries as well as Finland and Iceland. Indeed, if you refer to a Finnish person as Scandinavian, they will probably give you a lesson.

Many of the recipes in this cookbook are rooted in the Scandinavian baking traditions, so there are no Finnish or Icelandic recipes. Norway, Sweden, and Denmark do have separate cultural identities and histories, and there are baked goods specific to each of these three places. For instance, Danes eat the most rye bread, whereas Norwegians also regularly munch on lefse, a potato flatbread that can be enjoyed like a tortilla to scoop up savory food or spread with butter, sprinkle with sugar, and wrap up to be eaten as a dessert. Swedes make a soft flatbread, similar in texture to pita, with a dough that includes a variety of ground spices, and they top crispbread with butter and cheese and other toppings.

Because I spent fifteen years in Denmark, many of the recipes in this cookbook originate there. But over the years, I have been introduced to the foods and customs of the neighboring countries, through my own travels, the time spent at our summer house in Sweden, and from my Norwegian and Swedish friends in Denmark. Some of those friends (plus a few more Scandinavian friends that I made in the United States) have generously shared a sampling of recipes for their home-baked concoctions, and I have included my favorites of those.

While certain baked goods come from a specific Scandinavian country, like Æbleskiver (page 236) from Denmark or Lefse (page 171) from Norway, there is enough overlap in their baking styles and recipes that it's difficult to spell out significant differences between the three countries' baking cultures. They share a similar ingredient profile and a minimalist aesthetic, so grouping them together in a Scandinavian baking book makes sense to me.

The good news is that Scandinavian baking requires few special ingredients. If there is one flavor that most people claim "tastes Scandinavian," it would have to be cardamom. Cardamom is a spice used in many other cuisines, and historians trace its arrival in Scandinavia back to the Middle Ages, when the Moors settled in Spain and traders from the north got hold of the spice. Like cinnamon, nutmeg, ginger, and cloves, it is considered a "warming spice" (welcomed in this cold region) and makes an appearance in a plethora of Scandinavian baked goods.

THE SCANDINAVIAN PANTRY

The vast majority of the staple ingredients used in Scandinavian baking—like butter, sugar, eggs, and flour—are easy to find at just about any local supermarket and are likely to be in your cupboard or fridge already. That said, some of these recipes call for a few specialty ingredients that you may need or want to order online, where you could find less expensive or high-quality versions, as in the case of pearl sugar and decorticated cardamom. The following list includes those specialty ingredients worth stocking up on, as well as others used prominently throughout these recipes.

ALMOND PASTE

Nuts, especially almonds, are frequently used in Scandinavian baking, and almond paste is a go-to ingredient for creating nutty pastry fillings like those in Semlor (page 127) and Tebirkes (page 149). Almond paste is made from ground almonds and sugar, feels malleable like Play-Doh, and is sold in small quantities in the baking aisle of the grocery store. If you know that you're going to try a few of the recipes that include this ingredient, then you might want to buy one of the 1-pound (455 g) tubs by the brand Mandelin, which are available online. Once you've opened the tub, be sure to rewrap the unused portion tightly and then store it in the refrigerator to keep it from drying out. That way, it will stay fresh for about six months.

BUTTER

All of the recipes in this cookbook call for unsalted butter. For baking, this is always my preference, as it allows you to control the amount of added salt in the recipe. If you use salted butter, be sure to reduce (or eliminate) the salt called for in the recipe.

DECORTICATED CARDAMOM

The cardamom you buy at the supermarket comes in two forms, ground and in whole pods, neither of which are ideal. Ground cardamom that has been sitting in a jar for who knows how long often loses the majority of its appealingly astringent smell and taste. What you want are the seeds from the pods, but it's a headache to try and excavate them on your own, with a lot of labor yielding a depressingly small quantity. Thankfully, you can buy decorticated cardamom from gourmet spice shops or online, which means that someone

How to Fill a Piping Bag, page 228

else did the work of prying out the seeds from the pods, so all that's left for you to do is grind the quantity you need for your recipe. I like to use a mortar and pestle, but a spice grinder does the trick, too. I promise, one whiff of the freshly ground seeds and you will never go back to pre-ground again! If you use a mortar and pestle, begin by grinding the seeds in a circular motion and then pound them once they're crushed. (This will keep them from popping out.) Don't worry if you have some small bits and variation in size. Like flecks of vanilla bean in other baked goods, visible pieces of cardamom seeds will indicate that you're using the real deal. I buy spices from Penzeys, and I also like the brand the Spice Way, both of which sell cardamom seeds for a reasonable price. A little decorticated cardamom goes a long way. Remember: only grind what you need for each recipe, keeping the remainder of the seeds in a sealed container.

DRIED BEANS FOR BLIND BAKING

Blind baking means partially baking a raw pastry crust to ensure it stays crisp, without air bubbles or bulges, before you add the filling and finish baking it completely. To do this, press the rolled-out dough into the pan, then cover it with parchment paper and fill it with dried beans (or pie weights). The crust gets baked briefly, and the beans weigh it down, keeping the crust from bubbling. The dried beans can be cooled, stored, and used again and again for this process, so don't throw them out.

WHEAT FLOUR

Flours are often distinguished by their gluten content. Gluten is a natural protein that acts as a binder, holding food together and imparting stretchiness to dough. In general, the higher the gluten content, the stretchier the dough. Flour derived from wheat that has a high gluten content is sometimes called hard, whereas flour with a low gluten content is called soft. Bread flour (used in stretchy doughs like pizza dough) is a hard flour, averaging 13 to 14 percent gluten. Cake flour is a soft flour, averaging 7 to 9 percent gluten. All-purpose flour fits in between the two, coming in at around 12 percent gluten.

Flours made from American wheat typically have more gluten than Scandinavian wheat flour, so translating a recipe and making it work is more than just a linguistic challenge. While most of the recipes here call for all-purpose flour, there are a few that utilize a combination of different flours to achieve the right taste and texture, as in the recipe for Sprouted Rye Bread (page 198). The Danish Dough (page 135) that forms the base of so many of my favorite pastries requires bread flour, adding stability to the dough and the flaky, buttery layers.

The type of wheat flour that you use can make or break a recipe, so please pay attention to what type each recipe calls for. These recipes were all created using American flours so if you're baking from this book outside the US, keep an eye on the protein (gluten) level in your flour. Matching the flour called for in a recipe will help to produce baked goods that resemble the ones in this book. If you bake frequently, stock your pantry with a few varieties of flour. I recommend always having all-purpose flour, cake flour, and bread flour on hand (in addition to a small bag of rye flour).

LIGHT CORN SYRUP

Many Scandinavian baking recipes use a liquid sweetener, in the form of *lys sirup* (light syrup), made from sugar extracted from beets. The first sugar refinery came to Sweden in the seventeenth century, but for a long time even after that, granulated sugar as we know it today remained a costly luxury, beyond the reach of most Scandinavians, which is why a lot of recipes still use lys syrup instead. While it's an important ingredient to achieve the crisp yet chewy texture of things like Caramel Slices (page 47), "light syrup" is hard to find in the United States. However, light corn syrup gives baked goods the same taste and texture, so that's what I recommend in its place. If you avoid consuming corn syrup, try Lyle's golden syrup (imported from the United Kingdom and made from refined cane sugar) or brown rice syrup.

MALT SYRUP

Malt syrup is sometimes sold as "malted barley syrup." It is an essential ingredient in my Sprouted Rye Bread (page 198), imparting the right element of malted sweetness to the dough. It also goes into the syrup poured over the Brown Sugar "Focaccia" Cake (page 81). I typically buy the Eden brand, which is available online and at health food and gourmet grocery stores. In a pinch, brown rice syrup can be substituted, although you will lose some of the characteristic malted flavor.

RYE (FLOUR AND BERRIES)

As a crop, rye is tough and drought resistant, and it grows well in cooler climates. As a result, it is common in the northern parts of Scandinavia, where even the summers can be chilly. Rye flour has a pleasingly nutty and malted taste that makes it a delicious addition to breads and other baked goods, including cookies and cakes. I don't exclusively use rye flour in many of my recipes, as it has a tendency to produce dense and gummy baked goods because it doesn't have the same gluten power that wheat flours have. But by combining rye flour with gluten-strong flour types (like all-purpose or bread flour), your baked goods will benefit from the wonderful flavor of rye without the fussiness of baking with rye on its own. Both King Arthur and Bob's Red Mill sell rye flour that is available at well-stocked grocery stores. When possible, choose rye flour that is organic and stone ground. All rye flour should be stored in the refrigerator in an airtight container, where it will stay fresh for several months, or in the freezer, where it will keep for about six months. Cold air slows the oxidation process that can make flour taste rancid.

Rye kernels, usually referred to as rye berries, are the least processed form of rye, with only the hull (the outer husk) removed. In their raw form, they resemble grains of long-grain brown rice, with a slight greenish/bluish tinge. When sprouted, they soften and their flavor is surprisingly sweet and grassy. Sprouted rye berries are a key ingredient in Sprouted Rye Bread, as they add a chewiness and subtle sweetness to the bread. Most well-stocked grocery stores and health food stores will sell rye berries, often in a bulk section, and they are available online, too.

SWEDISH PEARL SUGAR

These crunchy little pellets of sugar resemble fat snowflakes that have magically landed on your baked goods. At Kantine, many customers mistake them for the kind of salt on soft pretzels. We sprinkle this unique sugar on sweets like our Cinnamon Knots (page 113) and Chocolate Slices (page 48) to add an authentic Swedish look as well as a tad of sweetness that (unlike regular sugar) will keep its pearly shape and won't dissolve during baking. A box of pearl sugar isn't very expensive, a little goes a long way, and it keeps indefinitely. Lars Own is a favorite brand, and it's available online and at some well-stocked grocery stores. Please don't mistakenly purchase Belgian pearl sugar, which resembles pea-size pieces of sugar that are designed to melt during baking and are often used in Belgian waffle batter.

VANILLA

Vanilla is not an afterthought in Scandinavian baking. Some of these buttery cookies and cakes, like the Vanilla Wreath Cookies (page 227), use vanilla as their prime flavoring agent. In this cookbook, we'll use whole vanilla beans in recipes in which seeing the black flecks and having a stronger vanilla-forward flavor adds something—for instance, in pastry cream. I use vanilla extract in doughs where extract imparts enough flavor and the flecks from a vanilla bean wouldn't be visible, so it doesn't seem worth the added expense.

Blackberry Tosca Cake, page 85

USEFUL BAKING EQUIPMENT

Many of the recipes here can be made with nothing more than an electric mixer (ideally a stand mixer, which comes in handy when kneading stiffer doughs), a baking tray, a whisk, and a spatula. However, if you want to take your Scandinavian baking to the next level, the following items are some of the tried-and-true tools I recommend having on hand. With them you'll be able to bake even more like a professional.

BENCH SCRAPER

A bench scraper is a flat rectangle made of steel with a handle on one edge, resembling the tool house painters use to apply putty. In fact, I bought a 6-inch putty knife at a hardware store and actually prefer it to the bench scraper I bought at a kitchen store because of its extra-thin blade. Bench scrapers have a variety of essential functions, from portioning and transferring hunks of dough from one place to another to removing stuck bits of dough from the counter without water so that you can immediately resume using it as a work surface. I also use mine to neaten the edges of pastry, as a knife, to mark lines when measuring, and to loosen rolled-out dough affixed to a countertop.

DIGITAL SCALE

Metric units reign in the Scandinavian kitchen and in the professional baking world as well, which is one reason we include them throughout this book. Baking requires precision, and scales are more precise than measuring cups. When you measure flour into a cup measure, the weight will vary based on whether you scoop directly from the bag or use a spoon to dump and level (as you should). But 120 grams of flour, weighed on a scale, will always be true. Similarly, wrappers on butter sticks may be printed with tablespoon markings, but that paper can slide, or you might just have a misshapen hunk of butter, so weighing your butter guarantees accuracy. Using a digital scale saves time and reduces the number of dishes to be washed, as dry ingredients can be poured directly into a mixing bowl set on the scale, rather than reaching for (and needing to rinse) a variety of measuring cups. Switching to a scale will instantly make you a more precise baker while simplifying your baking process. Once you start baking by weight, you'll never look back!

Scales are also essential for portioning dough. Ever wondered why cookies and buns at bakeries are so uniform in size? That's because professional bakers weigh the dough—pinching off a little here or adding a little there—to create baked goods of precisely the same size. Weighing scooped cookies or the dough to create specific pastries and buns will create a pleasing uniformity of shape and size to your baked goods, plus guarantee a uniform baking time.

INSTANT-READ THERMOMETER

An instant-read thermometer is very useful for serious baking, and is used to gauge the temperature of liquid before adding yeast, the temperature of a fermenting bread dough, as well as the internal temperature of a loaf of bread for doneness.

CAKE AND TART PANS WITH REMOVABLE BOTTOMS

There's nothing worse than a cake stuck in its pan, which is why I always, always bake layer cakes and tarts in pans with removable bottoms. I recommend purchasing two straight-sided 9-inch (23 cm) cheesecake-style or springform cake pans so that you can bake two layers at once. I also recommend a 9½-inch (24 cm) fluted tart pan with a removable bottom. The ruffled edge will make your Roasted Nut and Caramel Tart (page 94) and Summer Strawberry Tart with Custard and Chocolate (page 91) even prettier. If you already have a tart pan without a fluted edge, it will also do fine. If you have a cake or tart pan that has different dimensions, be aware that baking times may vary.

NOTCHED ROLLING PIN

A decorative notched rolling pin is used for rolling over Lefse (page 171), tunnbröd (page 173), and Rye Crispbread (page 175). This bumpy rolling pin leaves an attractive and authentic-looking pattern on the surface of rolled-out dough, and also helps to prevent air bubbles from forming during baking. Alternatively, you can roll out flatbreads with a regular rolling pin and then repeatedly prick the flattened surface of each with the tines of a fork instead. Notched rolling pins are available online, at many kitchen stores, and through purveyors of Scandinavian goods.

SPICE GRINDER OR COFFEE GRINDER

Grinding your own spices right before using them makes all the difference in creating flavorful and fragrant baked goods. I enjoy using a mortar and pestle to grind delicate spices like caraway seeds. But with bulkier spices, like cardamom seeds and star anise, a spice grinder gets the job done much more efficiently. If you don't have a grinder dedicated solely to spices, a coffee grinder wiped out with a dry towel will work just fine in a pinch.

OFFSET SPATULA

Inexpensive and useful for so many precise kitchen tasks, a small offset spatula (with a 4-inch / 10 cm blade) is one of my go-to tools. Mine are almost always either in use or dirty in the sink (which is why I have a few). I use them for spreading frosting, whipped cream, or melted chocolate. The offset blade allows you to smooth surfaces without your knuckles getting in the way. I also use it to level off cups of flour or sugar and to flip flatbreads and waffles while baking.

REUSABLE PASTRY BAG AND PIPING TIPS

Some of the recipes in this cookbook require a pastry bag and piping tip, an essential tool for filling buns with whipped cream, piping a Cake Person (page 97), and more. If you have never used one, have no fear. I will walk you through the process. While you can buy disposable plastic pastry bags, I recommend that you invest in a reusable canvas one as plastic bags tend to rip under pressure. Canvas pastry bags are lined with smooth plastic that makes them easy to rinse, dry, and reuse many times. My preference is a 16-inch (40 cm) canvas bag, which is large enough to accommodate plenty of dough, whipped cream, or other fillings but isn't unwieldy. Wilton is one brand that I like. For piping tips, I recommend one medium-size plain tip (Ateco #805 or similar) and one medium-size open star tip (Ateco #826 or similar).

STAND MIXER

If you are serious about baking, you might already have a stand mixer. A stand mixer is a tool that I can't imagine baking without. While a handheld mixer can be used to whip cream in a bowl, a stand mixer comes with a variety of tools besides the whisk that perform different tasks. The paddle attachment is invaluable for mixing cookie doughs and cake batters. The dough hook does an admirable job of kneading even the stiffest bread and pastry doughs. My home mixer is an old KitchenAid that has put up with more than twenty-five years of abuse!

Apple Dumplings with Buttermilk and Lemon Zest, page 236

STIFF RULER

A 12-inch (30 cm) ruler made of metal or clear, hard plastic is great to have handy in the kitchen. As nerdy as it may seem, a ruler ensures precision and better baking results, I promise! I use mine throughout the day for things like measuring the dough for Checkerboard Cookies (page 53), and Raspberry Squares (page 57), and straightening the edges of my Danish Dough (page 135) as I'm rolling it out. I recommend that you avoid wooden rulers in the kitchen, as they have a tendency to get nicked and lose their numbers over time, and are hard to keep clean.

HEART-SHAPED WAFFLE IRON

Dainty Scandinavian waffles are much thinner than the thick slabs of Belgium waffles, and they are most often made in a waffle iron that fashions the batter into five joined hearts. I keep my heart-shaped waffle iron out on the countertop as a reminder to use it when relaxing mornings permit a sweet touch. While this is not an essential tool, the waffles you make in one of these waffle irons, which are available online, will undoubtedly look and taste spot-on Scandinavian.

ÆBLESKIVER PAN

Æbleskiver, or apple dumplings, are made in a special pan that has a handle like a skillet (see photograph, opposite) but a cooking surface dimpled with egg-size wells. Traditionally these pans were made from cast iron but now can be found in lighter, nonstick aluminum versions. They can be purchased online and at thrift stores or garage sales. There's no way to make æbleskiver without one.

KRANSEKAKE MOLDS

The Marzipan Wreath Tower (page 239), a favorite confection for New Year's Eve or other celebratory times, is a stack of almond cookie rings of graduated sizes garnished ornately with piped royal icing, and sometimes small flags and streamers. The ring molds are available online and make the task of baking and building your own tower a lot easier than without.

BAKING BEST PRACTICES

Now that we've gone over baking tools, the next step is to have you moving like a baker, too. The following is a short list of my top tips for baking, honed over many years of working in restaurant kitchens and at home. These tips will serve you well when creating these Scandinavian baked goods, and odds are they will benefit other baking endeavors you embark on, too. Read through them, and although you may be familiar with a few already, a refresher never hurts. I've summarized some of these tips more succinctly within the body of the recipes that follow, but I wanted to spend a little time explaining the reasoning behind my advice and going into more detail about how to execute these procedures.

MEASURING FLOUR AND OTHER DRY INGREDIENTS

When using measuring cups, don't fill them directly from a bag or bin of flour, as this may compact the flour, causing you to use more than a recipe calls for. Instead, use a spoon to scoop flour into the measuring cup. Once the flour is mounded over the sides of the measuring cup, run the blunt side of a knife across the rim of the cup to scrape the excess flour back into your bin or bag.

Because there is still room for human error in this method, my preference is still always to use a scale to measure flour and other dry ingredients by weight (see page 29). It can be tricky to get an accurate weight on very small amounts such as teaspoons of salt or spices, so I use teaspoon and tablespoon measurements for small quantities.

MIXING BATTER

When baking cookies and cakes, you may notice that the general procedure for mixing the batter is fairly repetitive in terms of the order of steps. You typically start by "creaming" (or whipping) the wet ingredients—butter or oil and sugar(s) and possibly eggs—in a stand mixer before adding the separately whisked dry ingredients. While you can beat your wet ingredients for a fairly long time without any negative consequences, once you add the dry ingredients you should mix as lightly as possible to keep your cakes and cookies tender. I often turn off the mixer and do the last few stirs by hand, using a big rubber spatula to fully incorporate those last dusty traces of flour into the batter.

PROOFING DOUGH

Doughs for yeasted pastries like the buns and danishes in the "Let's Fika!" chapter require two separate resting periods. The first, often called a *rise*, comes immediately after forming the dough and usually takes around 1 to 2 hours on a countertop. This first rise can also be done overnight if you put the dough in a covered bowl or container in the refrigerator, where it can remain for up to 12 hours. The second resting period happens after you form the dough into whatever shape your pastry will take and is called a *proof* (a term that fans of *The Great British Bake Off* will surely know well!).

When I bake at home, I proof my shaped pastries in one of two ways: on the countertop (these instructions are included in the individual recipes) or in the oven, which creates an optimal environment for your unbaked pastries and therefore accelerates the proofing time. When I don't have to use my oven for something else, I opt for the oven proofing method.

To proof your unbaked pastries in the oven, place a small pot of freshly boiled water in one of the back corners of the unheated oven. Arrange two racks in the upper and lower thirds of the oven, then put the trays with your pastries on the racks. Be careful not to position the trays directly over the pot of hot water, or the butter in the pastry will melt out.

Proofing time varies for both methods, depending on whether the dough was room temperature or cold from the refrigerator prior to shaping. With countertop proofing in a warm kitchen environment, your pastries will need 1 to 2 hours, and when proofing in the oven, they will only need between 30 minutes to an hour before they are good to go. Proofed, ready-to-bake pastries should be noticeably puffier, and the impression of a fingerprint will be slow to fill in. (Over-proofing your pastries will results in flat, less flaky pastries.)

ROLLING OUT CRUST OR PASTRY DOUGH (THE "AIR HOCKEY" METHOD)

Whether you are rolling out dough for a buttery tart crust or Danish Dough (page 135), your dough is likely to stick to your work surface, especially if the temperature in your kitchen is warm. Here is my preferred method to keep the rolling-out process from becoming frustrating and the dough from turning into a sticky mess:

Visualize an air hockey puck, which should always skim the surface of the air hockey table. Similarly, you want your dough to stay separate from the work surface on which you are rolling it out, never letting it get glued down. To achieve this, as you roll out your dough, repeatedly lift it up as gently as you can, using your bench scraper to detach any stuck parts, and sprinkle just a bit of flour onto the work surface before continuing to roll it out. Doing this a few times will keep it from adhering to the surface. But work briskly so that your dough doesn't become too warm and sticky! If you need to use the same work surface to roll out more dough, use your bench scraper to scrape off any residual bits first so that you can start fresh, without the fear of your next batch sticking in the same spots.

PORTIONING DOUGH

To make buns of approximately the same size, I recommend forming your dough into equal-size logs, then cutting each log into pieces with a bench scraper. This method is much easier than tearing off pieces from one large blob of dough, and the bench scraper makes dividing, portioning, scooping, and transferring dough a lot easier.

WHIPPING CREAM

Whipped cream is a popular topping on Scandinavian cakes and in Scandinavian buns. The perfect whipped cream manages to be soft and luscious while still holding its shape, rather than collapsing. While whipping cream in the bowl of a stand mixer, most of us have probably had the unfortunate experience of waiting just a few seconds too long and seeing it turn clumpy as the fat and liquid in the cream begin to separate. To ensure that your whipped cream stays soft and cloudlike, I recommend whipping it as close to the time you'll be needing it as possible, and turning off the mixer just before it looks done. Then remove the bowl and the whisk attachment and whisk it (with the attachment) to perfection by hand. This way, you're in complete control with less chance of overwhipping. If the bowl to your stand mixer is available, chill it in the freezer until right before you need to whip the cream.

THE COOKIE TIN

My introduction to Scandinavian baking came in a royal blue tin. As a kid in Ohio, those iconic Royal Dansk tins would pop up without fail around the holidays, holding pleated paper sleeves of butter cookies that I loved to dig into. My favorites were the pretzel-shaped cookies sprinkled with fat sugar crystals. A close second were the pretty vanilla wreaths. My least favorite were the ones with the tiny, dried-out raisins: the last to be eaten, but still eaten!

When I first made my way to Copenhagen at eighteen, I only went for the summer. But when I returned in my late twenties, married a Dane, and spent my first winter in Scandinavia, I was amazed to find homemade versions of the cookies I'd grown up eating. Not only did people bake their own Vanilla Wreath Cookies (page 227), but they even had special tins or their homemade cookies.

The Scandinavian cookie tin is similar in function to the American cookie jar, but often decorated on the outside with pretty patterns or hyggelig images. This handy vessel keeps cookies fresh and allows people to quickly arrange a few cookies on a plate for any family or friends who happen to pop by to say hello. My mother-in-law and I soon grew so close that she wouldn't bother arranging cookies on a plate for me; she'd just open the tin and set it on the table. She knew me well enough to realize that I couldn't resist her cookies!

As a baking enthusiast (and lover of baked goods), I immediately recognized that these homemade cookies were infinitely tastier than their factory-made counterparts. I was hooked, not only on Danish cookies, but on this culture that clearly valued home baking and placed a priority on spending time together (always with freshly baked treats!).

Cookies hold a sacred place in Scandinavian baking. There is a tradition in Sweden, going back to the nineteenth century, called a kafferep, which means "coffee party," where pastries are served along with coffee. The funny part is that Sweden actually has a history of banning coffee, having done so five separate times. The notorious King Gustav III, who ruled Sweden in the 1770s, believed that coffee was a poison that shortened life spans and would imprison people for drinking excessive amounts. Swedish scholars corroborated this belief by arguing that coffee was toxic and contributed to digestive upset. In addition, it was considered "too foreign" by some early Swedes, who wanted to preserve a version of Swedish culture that existed before the bean was imported.

But as is often the case when something becomes contraband, prohibiting coffee only served to heighten its appeal for many people, who continued to drink the illicit substance. Once the bans were finally lifted, Swedes celebrated by throwing parties at which seven different types of cookies had to be served, typically including a "cave," like the jam-filled Black Currant Cave (page 44), a Checkerboard Cookie (page 53), an Oatmeal Lace Cookie (page 63), and chewy almond shortbread called Finska Pinnar (page 43).

While baking seven different types of cookies for a party might seem like a tall order, Scandinavian cookies are typically quite simple, made of just a handful of kitchen staples: butter, flour, sugar, and eggs, a spice or two, possibly some nuts or jam. Nonetheless, these recipes should be of interest to home bakers curious to try new things as they often feature unique forming or baking techniques.

All of the cookie recipes in this chapter come together quickly. Many can be mixed in one bowl and made ahead of time, allowing you to chill the dough to have ready to bake on demand. These cookies also store well, so you can fill your own tin or, what the heck, why not go all out and throw a traditional Swedish cookie party!

FINNISH ALMOND MATCHSTICKS

Finska Pinnar

Oddly, there is no evidence that these shortbread cookies come from Finland or that Finns eat them. But they are popular in Denmark, where most people probably already have the basic ingredients on hand to bake them when the urge strikes. In my version, I add almond flour to the dough, which makes them slightly soft and delightfully chewy. The result is simple but not boring, pretty without being fussy, a treat that's not too sweet: Scandinavian minimalism at its finest. MAKES 16 COOKIES

1 cup (226 g) unsalted butter, cold, cut into about 8 pieces

1 cup (200 g) sugar

2 cups (256 g) all-purpose flour

¾ cup (75 g) almond flour

1 teaspoon kosher salt

2 teaspoons vanilla extract

To finish

1 egg

2 tablespoons sliced almonds

In the bowl of a stand mixer fitted with the paddle attachment, combine the butter, sugar, all-purpose flour, almond flour, and salt and mix on low until it forms a coarse sand. Add the vanilla and mix again. This liquid should cause the dough to cohere into a ball.

Divide the dough into two equal portions. Wrap each portion in parchment paper or plastic wrap and chill for at least 30 minutes in the refrigerator. Because this dough doesn't contain eggs, it can be refrigerated safely at this point for up to 1 week if you want to make it ahead to bake later. The dough can also be frozen, either as the two portions (to be thawed and shaped later) or as matchsticks (see shaping directions below).

When ready to bake the cookies, line two 13 by 18-inch (33 by 46 cm) baking trays with parchment paper. Arrange two racks in the upper and lower thirds of the oven and preheat the oven to 350°F (175°C). After removing the dough from the refrigerator, you may need to work it with your hands to warm it up again so that it becomes flexible. Then roll each ball of dough into a 16-inch (40 cm) log. I don't flour my counter before doing this, but if you find that the dough is sticking, add just a pinch of flour to your work surface before proceeding. Cut each log into eight cookies at 2-inch (5 cm) intervals. These are your matchsticks. Try to keep the edges blunt. Arrange them on the prepared baking trays with 1 inch (2.5 cm) between.

In a small bowl, whisk the egg with a fork. Using a pastry brush, lightly brush the top of each cookie with the egg wash. Use your fingertips to break up the almonds and then sprinkle them over the cookies (smaller pieces will stick better).

Place the baking trays in the oven and bake for 10 to 12 minutes, rotating the baking trays halfway through from top to bottom and front to back, until light golden brown (especially at the edges). Transfer them to a rack to cool before serving. Store the cookies in an airtight container, where they will stay fresh for up to 4 days.

BLACK CURRANT CAVES

Svartvinbärsgrottor

Grottor, or "caves," are a popular Swedish cookie shape, essentially a Scandi-style thumbprint cookie. Most often these cookies are made with raspberry jam, but when I visited Denmark for the first time and tasted black currant jam on a piece of rye bread with butter, I fell in love with its sourness and distinctive, earthy flavor. These cookies put black currant jam to great use. After baking, the cookies taste like tiny black currant pies. Black currant jam is widely available at gourmet grocery stores and online. MAKES 16 COOKIES

1 cup plus 2 tablespoons (256 g) unsalted butter, at room temperature

1⁄3 cup (66 g) granulated sugar

1⁄3 cup (62 g) powdered sugar

3 egg yolks

1 teaspoon vanilla extract

3 cups (384 g) all-purpose flour, plus more for dusting

1½ teaspoons baking powder

1⁄4 teaspoon kosher salt

To finish

1 egg

1 tablespoon demerara sugar

3⁄4 cup (150 g) black currant jam

Line two 13 by 18-inch (33 by 46 cm) baking trays with parchment paper. Arrange two racks in the upper and lower thirds of the oven and preheat the oven to 350°F (175°C). In the bowl of a stand mixer fitted with the paddle attachment, beat the butter, granulated sugar, and powdered sugar on medium until soft and creamy, pausing halfway through to scrape the sides and bottom of the bowl with a rubber spatula, 2 to 3 minutes. Add the egg yolks and vanilla and mix until well blended.

In a large bowl, whisk together the flour, baking powder, and salt. Add the flour mixture to the butter mixture and mix until all the ingredients are well incorporated. The dough will be fairly thick.

Divide the dough into two equal portions. Lightly dust a work surface with flour, then roll each ball of dough into a log about 12 inches (30 cm) long. Cut each log into eight cookies at 1½-inch (3.5 cm) intervals and arrange them on the prepared baking trays, spaced 2 to 3 inches (5 to 7.5 cm) apart. Use your thumb to make a careful depression in the top of each cookie. Your thumb should come about 1⁄4 inch (6 mm) shy of the baking tray. Be careful not to push all the way through the dough. As you press down, the cookie will expand into a rounded shape. Don't worry if the edges of the dough crack a little.

In a small bowl, whisk the egg with a fork. Using a pastry brush, lightly brush each cookie with the egg wash, focusing on the edges. Sprinkle the tops with the demerara sugar.

Drop a heaping teaspoon of the jam into the center of each cookie.

Bake for 17 to 20 minutes, rotating the baking trays halfway through from top to bottom and front to back, until golden at the edges and the jam is set. Transfer them to a rack to cool completely. Store the cookies in an airtight container, where they will stay fresh for up to 3 days.

CARAMEL SLICES
Kolasnittar

Made from just a handful of basic pantry staples, this recipe yields a nearly foolproof cookie that is crisp and crackly on the outside with a chewy texture and caramel taste. The cookies get sliced right after they come out of the oven. The two rounded ends are always worth fighting for because—like the corners of a tray of brownies—they have the highest ratio of crisp edge to chewy center. While lots of variations of this Swedish cookie exist, this simple version is a personal favorite. MAKES 32 COOKIES

14 tablespoons (200 g) unsalted butter, at room temperature

1 cup (200 g) sugar

⅓ cup (100 g) light corn syrup

1½ teaspoons vanilla extract

2⅓ cups (298 g) all-purpose flour, plus more for dusting

1 teaspoon baking soda

1 teaspoon kosher salt

Line two 13 by 18-inch (33 by 46 cm) baking trays with parchment paper.

In the bowl of a stand mixer fitted with the paddle attachment, beat the butter, sugar, corn syrup, and vanilla on medium until soft and creamy, pausing halfway through to scrape the sides and bottom of the bowl with a rubber spatula, about 3 minutes.

In a large bowl, whisk together the flour, baking soda, and salt. Add the flour mixture to the butter mixture and mix on low speed until all the ingredients are well incorporated.

Form the dough into a ball, then divide it into four equal portions. Lightly dust a work surface with flour, then roll each portion into a log about 12 inches (30 cm) long.

Place two logs side by side, at least 3 inches (7 cm) apart, on each of the prepared baking trays. Using your fingertips, flatten the logs to about ½ inch (1 cm) thick and about 1½ inches (3.5 cm) wide. Ensure that there is at least 1 inch (2.5 cm) of space around each flattened log (or 2 inches/5 cm between the logs).

Refrigerate the dough on the baking trays for at least 30 minutes before baking. If you wish to bake them later, cover the trays with plastic wrap and store in the fridge for up to 3 days or in the freezer for up to 2 weeks. They can be baked directly from the freezer, but when doing so increase the baking time by 4 to 6 minutes.

To bake the cookies, arrange two racks in the upper and lower thirds of the oven and preheat the oven to 350°F (175°C). Bake for 16 to 18 minutes, rotating the baking trays halfway through from top to bottom and front to back, until uniformly golden and browned at the edges. The logs should be a little soft to the touch with a shiny and cracked surface.

While still hot and on the baking trays, cut each log into eight 1½-inch-wide (3.5 cm) slices on a diagonal. Transfer them to a rack to cool. Store the cookies in an airtight container, where they will stay fresh for up to 3 days.

CHOCOLATE SLICES

Chokladsnittar

A regular at Kantine refers to these Swedish cookies as "brownie sticks," and she dunks them in her coffee while eating—now try doing that with a regular brownie! MAKES 32 COOKIES

14 tablespoons (200 g) unsalted butter, at room temperature

1 cup (200 g) granulated sugar

⅓ cup (100 g) light corn syrup

2 eggs

2 teaspoons vanilla extract

2⅓ cups (256 g) all-purpose flour, plus more for dusting

⅓ cup (30 g) Dutch-processed cocoa powder

1 teaspoon baking powder

½ teaspoon kosher salt

To finish

4 tablespoons (60 g) Swedish pearl sugar (see page 25)

Line two 13 by 18-inch (33 by 46 cm) baking trays with parchment paper.

In the bowl of a stand mixer fitted with the paddle attachment, beat the butter, granulated sugar, and corn syrup on medium until soft and creamy, pausing halfway through to scrape the sides and bottom of the bowl with a rubber spatula, about 3 minutes. Add 1 of the eggs and the vanilla and mix again to incorporate.

In a large bowl, sift together the flour, cocoa powder, baking powder, and salt. Add the flour mixture to the butter mixture and mix on low speed until all the ingredients are well incorporated.

Form the dough into a ball and divide it into four equal portions. If the dough feels too soft to handle, wrap and chill it for 10 minutes. Lightly dust a work surface with flour, then roll each portion into a log about 12 inches (30 cm) long.

Place two logs side by side, at least 3 inches (7.5 cm) apart, on each of the prepared baking trays. Using your fingertips, flatten the logs to about ½ inch (1 cm) thick and about 1½ inches (3.5 cm) wide. Ensure that there is at least 1 inch (2.5 cm) of space around each log (or 2 inches/5 cm between the logs). In a small bowl, whisk the remaining egg. Using a pastry brush, brush each log with the egg wash. Sprinkle 1 tablespoon of the pearl sugar over each log.

Refrigerate the dough on the baking trays for at least 30 minutes before baking. If you wish to bake them later, cover the trays with plastic wrap and store in the fridge for up to 3 days or in the freezer for up to 2 weeks. They can be baked directly from the freezer, but when doing so increase the baking time by 4 to 6 minutes.

To bake the cookies, arrange two racks in the upper and lower thirds of the oven and preheat the oven to 350°F (175°C). Bake for 16 to 18 minutes, rotating the baking trays halfway through from top to bottom and front to back. The cookie's brown color can make it hard to judge doneness. Look for an overall puffiness and a dry edge. While they are still hot, cut each logs into eight 1½-inch-wide (3.5 cm) slices on a diagonal. Transfer them to a rack to cool. Store the cookies in an airtight container, where they will stay fresh for up to 3 days.

BLACK LICORICE SLICES

Lakritssnittar

Black licorice is divisive. Most people either hate it or love it, but those who love it can't get enough of it. Licorice is a popular flavor throughout Scandinavia. Most often it takes the form of candy, and grocery stores, gas stations, and convenience stores have racks filled with salty and sweet, hard and soft black licorice. Interestingly enough, there aren't a lot of recipes featuring black licorice as a flavor, and these cookies fill that gap. The dough gets it irresistible licorice flavor from three key ingredients: ground star anise, licorice root powder, and molasses. I also decorate them with chopped black licorice candy, which magically stays chewy after baking. Yet even with all that licorice, these cookies are subtle, intriguing, and addictive. They've been known to convert people who think they can't stand the stuff. **MAKES 32 COOKIES**

4 long ropes (about 2 oz/56 g) sweet black licorice (Panda or Wiley Wallaby brands are both good)

1 cup (226 g) unsalted butter, at room temperature

1 cup (200 g) sugar

⅓ cup (100 g) molasses

2½ cups (298 g) all-purpose flour, plus more for dusting

1 teaspoon baking soda

1 teaspoon ground star anise (from about 3 pods)

1 teaspoon licorice root powder (see Note, page 52)

1 teaspoon kosher salt

Line two 13 by 18-inch (33 by 46 cm) baking trays with parchment paper.

Chop the licorice into pea-sized pieces. Your knife may get sticky and need to be rinsed to keep the licorice from clumping. If it still clumps, pop the licorice into the freezer for a few minutes to stiffen it up. Set aside while you make the cookie dough.

In the bowl of a stand mixer fitted with the paddle attachment, beat the butter, sugar, and molasses on medium until soft and creamy, pausing halfway through to scrape the sides and bottom of the bowl with a rubber spatula, about 3 minutes.

In a large bowl, whisk together the flour, baking soda, star anise, licorice root powder, and salt. Add the flour mixture to the butter mixture and mix on low until just incorporated. Form the dough into a ball, then divide it into four portions of approximately the same size. If the dough feels too soft to handle, wrap it in parchment paper or plastic wrap and chill it in the refrigerator for a few minutes. Lightly dust a work surface with flour, then roll each portion into a log about 12 inches (30 cm) long.

Place two logs side by side, at least 3 inches (7.5 cm) apart, on each of the prepared baking trays. Using your fingertips, flatten the logs to about ½ inch (1 cm) thick and about 1½ inches (3.5 cm) wide. The dough will continue to spread while baking, so ensure that there is at least 1 inch (2.5 cm) of space around each flattened log (or 2 inches/5 cm between the logs).

CONTINUED

Evenly disperse the chopped licorice over the surface of each flattened log. Moisten your fingertips and press it in just slightly to keep it from rolling off.

Refrigerate the dough on the baking trays for at least 30 minutes before baking. If you wish to bake them later, cover the trays with plastic wrap and store in the fridge for up to 3 days or in the freezer for up to 2 weeks. They can be baked directly from the freezer, but when doing so increase the baking time by 4 to 6 minutes.

To bake the cookies, arrange two racks in the upper and lower thirds of the oven and preheat the oven to 350°F (175°C). Bake for 16 to 18 minutes, until darker at the edges, rotating the baking trays halfway through from top to bottom and front to back. The finished cookies should be slightly soft to the touch with a shiny and cracked surface.

While they are still hot, cut each log into eight 1½-inch-wide (3.5 cm) slices on a slight diagonal. Transfer them to a rack to cool. Store the cookies in an airtight container, where they will stay fresh for up to 3 days.

NOTE Licorice is a weed that grows across Europe and Asia. While licorice and anise taste similar, they come from different plants. We eat anise in the form of seeds, whereas edible licorice is a root that can be made into a powder and used as a spice. While it's not a common ingredient in American baking, raw licorice root is used in Ayurvedic medicine, and it can be found at health food stores and online. Starwest Botanicals makes an organic licorice root powder that works well in baked goods and candies.

CHECKERBOARD COOKIES

Schackrutor

Checkerboard cookies, made from a grid of chocolate and vanilla shortbread, are one of the seven cookie varieties at traditional Swedish cookie parties. These pretty and impressive-looking cookies are not hard to make as long as you follow the steps and use a ruler for precision. The two differently colored doughs are made from one base dough, and cocoa powder is added to half. Be sure to allow time for chilling at different stages, which keeps your checkerboard pattern sharp. Like many traditional Scandinavian cookies, these checkerboards are on the small side, which means you can fit more in your tin (or pop more in your mouth). MAKES ABOUT 36 COOKIES

- 1 cup (226 g) unsalted butter, at room temperature
- ½ cup (100 g) granulated sugar
- ⅓ cup (41 g) powdered sugar
- 1 egg
- 1 egg yolk
- 1 teaspoon vanilla extract
- ½ teaspoon kosher salt
- 3 cups (288 g) all-purpose flour
- ⅓ cup (36 g) cocoa powder

Line a 13 by 18-inch (33 by 46 cm) baking tray with parchment paper.

In the bowl of a stand mixer fitted with the paddle attachment, beat the butter, granulated sugar, and powdered sugar on medium until soft and creamy, pausing halfway through to scrape the sides and bottom of the bowl with a rubber spatula, 2 to 3 minutes. Add the egg, egg yolk, vanilla, and salt and mix on medium until smooth.

With the mixer off, add the flour, then mix on low until just combined. You may want to drape a dish towel around the mouth of the mixing bowl at first to keep the flour contained.

Form the dough into a ball and then divide it into two equal portions, using your digital scale to ensure they are the same size. Return one portion to the bowl and add the cocoa powder. Mix on low speed until the cocoa is well incorporated (this will be your chocolate portion). Turn the dough out onto a work surface and knead it a few times to form a smooth ball that's uniform in color.

Working on the prepared baking tray, shape each ball of dough into a 2 by 6-inch (5 by 15 cm) rectangular slab, using a ruler for precision. Refrigerate the dough for at least 1 hour.

Slice each slab of dough lengthwise into thirds. Then rotate the dough 90 degrees on its long edge and cut it lengthwise into thirds again, for a total of nine strips per dough color.

CONTINUED

On a new sheet of parchment paper, lay one chocolate strip next to one vanilla strip next to one more chocolate strip. Top these three strips with another layer of strips of alternating colors, starting with vanilla. Finish with a third layer, again of alternating colors, starting with chocolate. You should end up with a 3-inch (7.5 cm) square log. Build a second log with the remaining dough, but start the first layer with two strips of vanilla dough and one strip of chocolate. You will end up with two checkerboard logs, one with vanilla corners, the other with chocolate corners. Using your fingertips, gently but firmly press the strips together, doing your best to preserve the squared edges. Put the slabs on a baking sheet and chill for at least 30 minutes in the refrigerator before slicing and baking.

Preheat the oven to 350°F (175°C).

Cut each log into 18 cookies at ¼-inch (0.5 cm) intervals and arrange them on the prepared baking tray, spaced 1 inch (2.5 cm) apart. Bake for 9 to 10 minutes, rotating the baking tray halfway through, until their surfaces are slightly puffed and dry looking and the vanilla squares look slightly golden. Let them cool on the baking tray for 1 to 2 minutes, until they have firmed enough to transfer to a rack to cool completely. Store the cookies in an airtight container, where they will stay fresh for up to 3 days.

RASPBERRY SQUARES

Hindbærsnitter

In this popular Danish cookie, a thick layer of fresh raspberry jam is spread between two large sheets of shortbread, and the top is drizzled with lemony royal icing before it's cut into squares and sprinkled with freeze-dried raspberries. When raspberries are in season, I like to make my own raspberry jam, with less sugar than most commercial varieties, which lets the taste of the fruit shine. If you don't have time to make the jam, I recommend crushing ½ cup of fresh raspberries and mixing it into 1 cup of store-bought raspberry jam for a fresher, more fruit-forward taste. When buying jam, look for a low-sugar, high-fruit brand. MAKES 9 COOKIES

Raspberry jam

2 cups (250 g) raspberries, fresh or thawed frozen

½ cup (100 g) granulated sugar

1 tablespoon fresh lemon juice

Shortbread sheets

1¼ cups (160 g) all-purpose flour

1½ cups (200 g) cake flour

1 cup (125 g) powdered sugar

½ teaspoon kosher salt

1 cup (226 g) cold unsalted butter, diced

1 egg

1 teaspoon vanilla extract

Lemony royal icing

1 cup (125 g) powdered sugar

Juice and zest of ½ lemon

1 to 2 teaspoons water, if needed

To finish

1 cup freeze-dried raspberries

MAKE THE JAM

In a medium saucepan over medium heat, add the berries, sugar, and lemon juice. Bring the mixture to a simmer and cook until reduced and thickened slightly, stirring occasionally, about 10 minutes. Pour the jam into a small bowl and refrigerate until chilled. If not using immediately, the jam will keep in an airtight container for up to 1 week in the refrigerator.

MAKE THE SHORTBREAD SHEETS

In a food processor, pulse the flour, cake flour, powdered sugar, and salt a few times, until just blended. Add the butter and pulse about five to ten times, until it forms a coarse sand. Add the egg and pulse to combine. Then add the vanilla and pulse until the sand-like pieces of dough cohere into one clump.

Divide the dough into two equal portions, using your digital scale to ensure they're the same size. Wrap each portion in parchment paper or plastic wrap and refrigerate for at least 30 minutes, or up to overnight.

When you are ready to bake the shortbread sheets, arrange two racks in the upper and lower thirds of the oven and preheat the oven to 350°F (175°C).

Place one portion of the dough on a piece of parchment paper and place a second piece of parchment paper on top (the dough has a tendency to stick to the rolling pin, so rolling it out between two sheets of parchment paper will be easier). Roll the dough into a 9-inch (23 cm) square, ensuring a uniform thickness. Repeat with the second portion of dough.

CONTINUED

Remove the top layer of parchment paper and use a ruler or bench scraper to neaten the edges and square off the corners. Transfer each shortbread sheet, with the bottom layer of parchment paper still underneath, to a 13 by 18-inch (33 by 46 cm) baking tray. Prick both sheets all over with the tines of a fork, at least twenty times each, to keep them from puffing.

Bake the shortbread for 15 minutes or until the edges have begun to brown, rotating the baking trays halfway through from top to bottom and front to back. You want the shortbread to be baked through but not crispy, so that it doesn't shatter when you cut it. Transfer the shortbread, still on the parchment paper, to a rack to cool. While the shortbread bakes, make the lemony royal icing.

MAKE THE ICING

In a medium bowl, whisk together the powdered sugar, lemon juice, and lemon zest. Your icing should have the consistency of thick honey. If needed, add the water to thin it.

ASSEMBLE

Once the shortbread has cooled completely, transfer both layers to a flat work surface or tray. Use a rubber spatula to spread the jam evenly across the surface of one of the shortbread sheets. With a small offset spatula, spread the icing evenly across the surface of the second shortbread sheet. With your fingers, crumble the freeze-dried raspberries over the icing while it is still wet. Very carefully lift the icing-covered shortbread sheet and place it neatly on top of the jam-covered sheet, icing side up. Let them rest for about an hour while the icing dries and hardens.

Using a long serrated knife and a gentle sawing motion, carefully cut the sandwiched shortbread into nine 3-inch (7.5 cm) squares. These are best within 1 day of baking, before the jam seeps through and makes them soggy.

HAZELNUT COOKIES

Nötkakor

If you love hazelnuts, these Swedish cookies will be right up your alley—crisp at the edges and moist and chewy at the center. My Swedish girlfriend Paula Holm told me her grandmother always made them as one of the seven types of cookies (!) she'd serve when she invited family over for coffee. And with only five ingredients, they can be made in a heartbeat. **MAKES 18 COOKIES**

2 cup (250 g) whole hazelnuts

2 eggs

1 cup (200 g) sugar

2½ teaspoons cornstarch

Pinch of kosher salt

Line a 13 by 18-inch (33 by 46 cm) baking tray with parchment paper and preheat the oven to 400°F (200°C).

In a food processor, pulse 1¾ cups (187 g) of the hazelnuts to a coarse sand, being careful not to turn them into nut butter.

In a large bowl, whisk the eggs. Add the ground hazelnuts, sugar, cornstarch, and salt and stir until it forms a fairly wet dough.

Drop the dough by the tablespoonful onto the prepared baking tray in three rows of six cookies each, spacing them about an inch (2.5 cm) apart. Using the remaining ¼ cup (63 g) hazelnuts, place a whole hazelnut in the center of each cookie.

Bake for 8 to 10 minutes, rotating the baking tray halfway through, until they are golden brown around the edges, puffy, and still slightly soft on top. Let the cookies cool completely before transferring them to a rack or plate, as they will be too soft to move while hot. Store the cookies in an airtight container, where they will stay fresh for up to 3 days.

RYE CHOCOLATE CHUNK COOKIES

Does anyone really need another chocolate chip cookie recipe? The answer is simple: Yes! This Kantine favorite embodies the essence of a quintessential chocolate chip cookie, with a touch of "Scandi-ness" thanks to the inclusion of rye flour and almond paste. The rye flour adds a hint of malt, the almond paste makes the insides of the cookies soft and gooey, and the heaps of chocolate chunks render them (does it even need saying?) irresistible when eaten warm and melty from the oven. MAKES 24 COOKIES

1 cup (226 g) unsalted butter, at room temperature

⅔ cup (135 g) packed light brown sugar

¾ cup (150 g) granulated sugar

1 egg

1½ teaspoons vanilla extract

⅔ cup (150 g) almond paste (see page 21)

2 cups (256 g) all-purpose flour

1 cup (106 g) rye flour (see page 25)

1 teaspoon baking soda

¾ teaspoon kosher salt

10 ounces (283 g) 63% (or higher) bittersweet chocolate, coarsely chopped

Line two 13 by 18-inch (33 by 46 cm) baking trays with parchment paper. Arrange two racks in the upper and lower thirds of the oven and preheat the oven to 350°F (175°C).

In the bowl of a stand mixer fitted with the paddle attachment, beat the butter, brown sugar, and granulated sugar on medium until soft and creamy, pausing halfway through to scrape the sides and bottom of the bowl with a rubber spatula, 2 to 3 minutes. Add the egg and vanilla, then beat on medium to fully combine. Add the almond paste and mix for another 2 minutes. It's okay if the paste isn't entirely integrated into the mixture, as any larger chunks will melt as the cookies bake.

In a large bowl, whisk together the flour, rye flour, baking soda, and salt. Add the flour mixture to the butter mixture and mix on low until all the ingredients are well incorporated. Add in the chocolate chunks and mix until just combined.

Portion the dough into golf ball–size scoops (about 65 g each). Flatten each one slightly between your palms and place them on the prepared baking trays, 2 to 3 inches (5 to 7.5 cm) apart.

Bake for 20 to 25 minutes, rotating the baking trays halfway through from top to bottom and front to back, until they are brown at the edges and the tops are still slightly soft. They will continue to firm up after you take them out of the oven, and to ensure that they stay soft and chewy, it's better to underbake them slightly rather than overbake. Let them cool on the baking trays for 1 to 2 minutes, until they have firmed enough to transfer to a rack to then cool completely. Store the cookies in an airtight container, where they will stay fresh for up to 3 days.

NOTE Chop bars of dark chocolate with a large serrated (bread-slicing) knife. That's the easiest way to keep it from flying around on the cutting board, and yields pieces with different shapes and sizes, resulting in a glorious chocolate chunk (vs. a more generic chocolate chip) cookie.

OATMEAL LACE COOKIES WITH CHOCOLATE

Havreflarn med Choklad

These Swedish oatmeal cookies are thin, crispy, and closer in texture to florentines than the thick-and-chewy oatmeal cookies popular in the United States. The butter, sugar, and bits of oat caramelize in the oven, forming a lacy texture. Be sure to use quick oats (oats that have been broken up). While these cookies can be enjoyed as is, sandwiching a layer of melted dark chocolate between two of them makes them irresistible. They also work well for ice cream sandwiches. These cookies stay fresh and hold their crispness for a while, so they're great to send in the mail. MAKES 30 COOKIES OR 15 CHOCOLATE SANDWICH COOKIES

1½ cups (167 g) quick oats

¾ cup (150 g) sugar

2 tablespoons all-purpose or gluten-free flour

1 teaspoon baking powder

¼ teaspoon kosher salt

½ cup (113 g) unsalted butter

1 egg

1 teaspoon vanilla extract

3 ounces (85 g) 63% (or higher) bittersweet chocolate, coarsely chopped (see Note, page 60)

Line two 13 by 18-inch (33 by 46 cm) baking trays with parchment paper. Arrange two racks in the upper and lower thirds of the oven and preheat the oven to 350°F (175°C).

In a large bowl, whisk together the oats, sugar, flour, baking powder, and salt.

In a small saucepan over medium heat, melt the butter. Immediately pour the melted butter into the flour mixture and stir to combine. Add the egg and vanilla and stir until it forms a dough.

Drop the dough by the teaspoonful (or using a small cookie scoop) onto the prepared baking trays, spaced about 1 inch (2.5 cm) apart.

Bake for 6 to 8 minutes, rotating the baking trays halfway through from top to bottom and front to back, until golden brown. Let them cool on the baking trays for 5 minutes, until they have firmed enough to transfer to a rack to then cool completely.

While the cookies are cooling, place the chocolate in a medium heat-resistant bowl. Fill a saucepan with 1 inch of water and bring to a low simmer. Place the bowl over (but not touching) the simmering water. Stir the chocolate occasionally until almost entirely melted. Remove bowl from saucepan and stir to melt any remaining bits. (Alternatively, you can melt your chocolate in the microwave at 50% power.)

To assemble the sandwich cookies, take one cookie and hold it flat side up. Using a small offset spatula, spread a ½ teaspoon or so of melted chocolate across the surface of the cookie in a thin layer and then top it immediately with a second cookie (flat side down) to form a sandwich. Place it back on the rack and repeat with the remaining cookies and chocolate. Store the cookies in an airtight container, where they will stay fresh for up to 5 days.

SAFFRON RUSKS

Saffransskorpor

This recipe comes from my dear friend Line Schou, a Swede living in Copenhagen. She introduced me to rusks, which are dry and crunchy biscuits, twice baked like biscotti, a common cookie in both the United Kingdom and Scandinavia. Babies often teethe on plain versions, while kids like to eat them as an after-school snack topped with butter and jam or cheese. Rusks stay crunchy for a couple of weeks, and are the perfect biscuit to dunk into tea or coffee. The addition of saffron here elevates the humble rusk, tinting the dough yellow and turning this commonplace cookie into something unexpectedly luxurious. These are delicious as is or with a schmear of cold butter. MAKES 40 SMALL COOKIES

½ cup (113 g) unsalted butter, at room temperature

1½ teaspoons (1.5 g) saffron threads

3 eggs

¾ cup (150 g) sugar, plus 2 tablespoons more for sprinkling

2⅔ cups (340 g) all-purpose flour

1½ teaspoons baking powder

½ teaspoon kosher salt

¾ cup (80 g) coarsely chopped hazelnuts

In a small saucepan over medium-high heat, melt the butter. Remove the pan from the heat and stir in the saffron. Let the saffron bloom in the melted butter for at least 30 minutes, until the butter has turned orange.

Line a 13 by 18-inch (33 by 46 cm) baking tray with parchment paper and preheat the oven to 375°F (190°C).

In the bowl of a stand mixer fitted with the paddle attachment, beat the eggs and the butter-saffron mixture on medium until combined. Turn off the mixer and add ¾ cup (150 g) of the sugar, the flour, baking powder, salt, and hazelnuts and mix on low for another 2 to 3 minutes, until a sunny yellow dough forms.

Divide the dough into two equal portions. Lightly dust a work surface with flour and then roll each portion into a 12-inch-long (30 cm) log. Place the logs side by side, 1 to 2 inches (2.5 to 5 cm) apart, on the prepared baking tray. Sprinkle the remaining 2 tablespoons of sugar onto the logs. Bake for 20 minutes, rotating the baking tray halfway through, until slightly puffed and firm to the touch.

Remove the baking tray from the oven and decrease the temperature to 250°F (120°C).

Let the logs cool on the baking tray. Using a sharp knife, cut each log into about twenty cookies at ½-inch (1 cm) intervals and arrange them on the same baking tray. Bake the cookies for an additional 40 minutes, rotating the baking tray halfway through, until the cookies are browned at the edges and hard. Store the cooled rusks in an airtight container, where they will stay fresh for up to 2 weeks.

SIMPLE CAKES AND CELEBRATION DESSERTS

I love to throw a dinner party. Little brings me more joy than having people I care about over for a relaxing evening in my home and serving them a meal cooked with care. These days, running a restaurant and raising my kids leaves little time for this sort of leisurely entertaining. However, when I do get the chance, I still go to the trouble of making one of the homemade desserts you'll see in the pages that follow—partly because it's not very much trouble at all.

If you can bake a cake from a mix, you can bake one from scratch. At least, you can bake these cakes, many of which require little more than mixing dry ingredients in one bowl, beating butter and sugar and eggs in another, and combining the two. One fuss-free cake that I especially love is the Lemon Moon Cake (page 73), a favorite among my Danish friends. The Cardamom-Scented Pear and Apple Snacking Cake (page 76) is another one-pan cake that pairs perfectly with an afternoon cup of coffee or tea.

Several of these cake recipes include a baked topping, eliminating the need for any kind of frosting. To make the Coconut Dream Cake (page 71), the batter gets partially baked before it's covered with a coconut topping and returned to the oven where it caramelizes to perfection. The Blackberry Tosca Cake (page 85) features a top layer of crunchy almond praline, which hides fresh blackberries, suspended in the cake underneath. These are cakes worthy of any celebration, but they look (and taste) like you went to more trouble to make them than you actually did.

Some of these recipes will introduce bakers to techniques that may be new. If you've never baked a yeasted cake, be sure to try the Brown Sugar "Focaccia" Cake (page 81). A pan of sweet dough gets topped with a brown sugar and butter glaze that fills the hollows you make by poking its yeasted surface with your fingertips. This recipe, from the Danish isle of Funen, is as much fun to make as it is delectable and unique.

You will notice that Scandinavian desserts almost always celebrate seasonality. Winter desserts are often built of nuts, caramel, and warming spices, whereas summer desserts almost always feature fresh fruit—typically the berries that flourish in Scandinavia during those warmer months. Of course, all of the fruits listed in these recipes are just suggestions. Feel free to substitute other fruits that might be in season or look especially good wherever you live.

COCONUT DREAM CAKE

Drømmekage

Coconut dream cake is a Danish favorite, typically eaten as a sweet snack. I've never been to a Danish potluck where there wasn't at least one dream cake on the table. A dense layer of coconut topping gets baked directly onto a rich butter cake, forming a chewy macaroon-like crown. While Danish grocery stores sell boxes of dream cake mix in the baking aisle, they will never, ever be as good as the homemade kind! Although this recipe is for a sheet cake (the most common way you'll find it in Denmark), you can also use it to make cupcakes. But remember to adjust your baking time accordingly. **MAKES ONE 9 BY 13-INCH (23 BY 33 CM) CAKE, OR 12 CUPCAKES**

Coconut topping

1 cup (226 g) unsalted butter

4 cups (200 g) unsweetened flaked or shredded coconut

2 cups (375 g) packed light brown sugar

¼ cup (59 g) whole milk

¾ teaspoon kosher salt

Cake

1 cup (226 g) unsalted butter, at room temperature, plus more for greasing

1¾ cups (375 g) granulated sugar

3 eggs

1 tablespoon vanilla extract

1½ cups (415 g) plain yogurt (preferably full-fat)

2½ cups (320 g) all-purpose flour, plus more for dusting if needed

→ INGREDIENTS CONTINUED

MAKE THE COCONUT TOPPING

In a large saucepan, combine the butter, coconut, brown sugar, milk, and salt. Place the pan over medium heat and stir the mixture continuously until the butter has just melted, 1 to 2 minutes. Set aside to cool.

MAKE THE CAKE

Butter a 9 by 13-inch (23 by 33 cm) baking pan, line the bottom with parchment paper, and preheat the oven to 350°F (175°C).

In the bowl of a stand mixer fitted with the paddle attachment, beat the butter and granulated sugar on medium until soft and creamy, 2 to 3 minutes. Add the eggs, one at a time, and mix until they are incorporated. Add the vanilla and yogurt, mixing to combine. Pause to scrape the sides and bottom of the bowl with a rubber spatula and then beat again for about 1 minute.

In a large bowl, whisk together the all-purpose flour, almond flour, baking powder, baking soda, and salt. Add the flour mixture to the mixer and beat on low until just combined.

Pour the batter into the prepared pan, smoothing it out with a rubber spatula. Bake for 40 to 45 minutes, until the cake is about three-quarters baked, firm enough that the coconut topping won't sink to the bottom after you add it. The cake should look golden on top, with cracks running down it, but still be slightly wobbly. A toothpick inserted in the center of the cake should come out with some batter on it.

Carefully remove the cake from the oven, leaving the oven on, and scatter spoonfuls of the coconut topping onto the cake. Do this gently (the cake will still be fragile).

CONTINUED

½ cup (48 g) almond flour

2 teaspoons baking powder

½ teaspoon baking soda

½ teaspoon kosher salt

Use an offset spatula to spread the topping evenly across the surface and out to the edges of the cake. Work swiftly, and don't sweat it if your topping is a bit clumpy; it will level out quite a bit as it bakes. Bake for 25 to 30 minutes more, until a toothpick inserted in the center of the cake comes out clean. The coconut topping will appear bubbly and darker brown at the edges, and the center will be a golden caramel color.

Remove the cake from the oven and use a butter knife to loosen the edges where the coconut topping is stuck to the sides of the pan. This makes cutting it easier after it cools. Once the cake is completely cooled, cut it into twelve to sixteen squares and serve them straight from the pan, being mindful of the parchment paper on the bottom. The cake can be made ahead; store it in an airtight container, where it will stay fresh for up to 3 days.

TO MAKE CUPCAKES Generously butter and flour a 12-cup muffin tin, making sure to coat all the flat surfaces between each cup with butter as well to prevent the coconut topping from sticking if your cakes overflow while baking. Decrease the initial baking time to 25 minutes, then add the coconut topping and bake for an additional 20 minutes, testing for doneness with a toothpick. Immediately after removing the cupcakes from the oven, use a butter knife to loosen the edges of each one, wherever the batter has come into contact with the pan. Then wait until the cupcakes cool completely before removing them.

LEMON MOON CAKE

Citronmåne

In Denmark, citronmåne is a popular commercially produced lemon cake that is factory baked in round cake pans, cut in half down the middle, and sold wrapped in plastic at the supermarket. This supermarket cake is full of preservatives, but it's something that Danes have been eating for decades, so it tastes like home to them.

My Danish husband worked in the television industry for a number of years. A while back he was in the Philippines with a Danish TV crew. They were all feeling a bit homesick when a cameraman suddenly disappeared into his tent and came back with a lemon moon cake, still in its plastic wrapper. He had brought it from Denmark stowed in his suitcase, waiting for the perfect moment to bring it out. Thanks to the endless string of additives and preservatives on the label, it was still so moist and full of lemony zing that you would've thought it had been baked that very day. While there is something to be said for an indestructible cake when you're on the road, this version, made from scratch, is much tastier: extra lemony with lots of zest and juice in both the cake and the glaze.

This recipe is inspired by the lemon moon cakes that our head baker, Hannah Jacobson, makes at Kantine. She had never heard of these cakes before starting with us, yet her cakes are true to the very best homemade version I ever tasted while living in Scandinavia and are exponentially better than any store-bought one.

The recipe makes one round cake. Cut it in half to form two cakes if you want the Danish half-moon shape, but if you prefer a full moon, I won't tell! **MAKES ONE 9-INCH (23 CM) CAKE**

Cake

- 1 cup (226 g) unsalted butter, at room temperature, plus more for greasing
- 4 lemons (Eureka lemons are typical, but Meyer lemons would make a fun variation)
- 1 cup plus 1 tablespoon (220 g) sugar
- 4 eggs
- ⅓ cup (100 g) almond paste (see page 21)
- 1 teaspoon vanilla extract

→ INGREDIENTS CONTINUED

MAKE THE CAKE

Butter a 9-inch (23 cm) round cake pan and line the bottom with parchment paper. Preheat the oven to 325°F (165°C).

Zest all 4 lemons into a small bowl and set aside. Juice the lemons into a measuring cup (you should have about ½ cup/155 g) and set aside as well.

In the bowl of a stand mixer fitted with the paddle attachment, beat the butter and sugar on medium until soft and creamy, pausing halfway through to scrape the sides and bottom of the bowl with a rubber spatula, 2 to 3 minutes. Add the eggs, one at a time, and mix until pale and creamy. Add the almond paste and vanilla, mixing to combine. Pause to scrape the sides and bottom of the bowl with a rubber spatula and then beat again for about 1 minute.

In a large bowl, whisk together the flour, almond flour, baking powder, and salt. Add the flour mixture to the mixer and mix on low until just

combined. Then add the lemon zest and half the lemon juice (about ¼ cup/59 g), reserving the rest for the glaze.

Place the prepared pan on an unlined baking tray and pour in the batter, smoothing it out with a rubber spatula. Bake for 1 hour, until the surface looks slightly puffed with a few brown spots and a toothpick inserted in the center of the cake comes out clean; if it doesn't, bake for 5 to 10 minutes more. Allow the cake to cool completely on a rack before removing it from the pan and glazing.

2 cups (256 g) all-purpose flour

½ cup (45 g) almond flour

1 teaspoon baking powder

½ teaspoon kosher salt

Lemon glaze

1½ cups (160 g) powdered sugar, plus more as needed

Fresh lemon juice, if needed

1 teaspoon unsalted butter, melted

Small pinch of kosher salt

WHILE THE CAKE IS BAKING, MAKE THE GLAZE

In a medium bowl, combine the powdered sugar, the remaining juice (about ¼ cup/59 g), the butter, and the salt. Whisk everything together until smooth, making sure there are no lumps. Because this makes such a small amount of glaze, this is easier to do by hand. If you're using a stand mixer, use the whisk attachment and be sure to pause to scrape the sides and bottom of the bowl with a rubber spatula, making sure to get under the whisk. The glaze should have the consistency of glue. If it's too runny, adjust by adding more powdered sugar. If it's too thick, add more lemon juice, 1 teaspoon at a time.

When the cake has cooled, remove it from the pan, cut it in half, then pour the glaze over it. Use a spatula to spread it across the surface and out to the edges of the cake, allowing it to drip a little over the cut edge.

The cake can be made ahead; store it in an airtight container in the refrigerator, where it will stay fresh for up to 3 days. Allow it to come to room temperature before eating.

CARDAMOM-SCENTED PEAR AND APPLE SNACKING CAKE

This snacking cake epitomizes fall. In the autumn, apples and pears grow abundantly in Scandinavia, and people often put baskets out on the curb to give away the surplus. I was delighted to find that many varieties of apples and pears also thrive in the Bay Area, so I could keep baking my go-to fall recipes from Scandinavia. In California, I also noticed piles of yellow quinces at the farmers' market in the fall, and I developed a version of the cake using poached quince and pears (see opposite). It's equally good with the more commonly available apples and pears. Cut small, the chunks of apple and pear soften while baking, and cardamom adds a distinctly Scandinavian flavor. MAKES ONE 9-INCH (23 CM) CAKE

½ cup (113 g) unsalted butter, at room temperature, plus more for greasing

¾ cup (150 g) granulated sugar

½ cup (100 g) packed light brown sugar

1 teaspoon freshly ground decorticated cardamom (see page 21)

2 eggs

1 egg yolk

2 teaspoons vanilla extract

¾ cup (100 g) whole wheat flour

¾ cup (100 g) cake flour

1½ teaspoons baking powder

1 teaspoon kosher salt

½ cup (150 g) sour cream

1 small pear, peel on, cut into ½-inch (1 cm) pieces

1 small apple, peel on, cut into ½-inch (1 cm) pieces

To finish

2 tablespoons cardamom sugar (see opposite)

Crème fraîche for serving (optional)

Butter a 9-inch (23 cm) cake pan and line the bottom with parchment paper. Preheat the oven to 350°F (175°C).

In the bowl of a stand mixer fitted with the paddle attachment, beat the butter, granulated sugar, brown sugar, and cardamom on medium until soft and creamy, pausing halfway through to scrape the sides and bottom of the bowl with a rubber spatula, 2 to 3 minutes. Add the eggs, one at a time, then the egg yolk, and mix until they are incorporated. Add the vanilla and mix to combine. Pause to scrape the sides and bottom of the bowl again, then beat for about 1 minute more.

In a large bowl, whisk together the whole wheat flour, cake flour, baking powder, and salt. Add the flour mixture to the mixer and mix on low until just combined. Increase the speed to medium, add the sour cream, and beat for about 1 minute more, until well blended.

Place the prepared pan on an unlined baking tray and pour in the batter, smoothing it out with a rubber spatula. Distribute the pear and apple chunks evenly on top of the batter. Sprinkle the cardamom sugar on top of the fruit.

Bake for 50 minutes to 1 hour, until the top and edges are dark golden brown and a toothpick inserted in the center of the cake comes out clean; if it doesn't, bake for 5 to 10 minutes more. Allow the cake to cool for 10 minutes before removing it from the pan. Serve slices warm or at room temperature with a small spoonful of crème fraîche (if desired).

The cake can be made ahead; store it in an airtight container in the refrigerator, where it will stay fresh for 2 to 3 days. Allow it to come to room temperature before eating. This cake is a good one to send in the mail.

CARDAMOM SUGAR

Cardamom sugar is a staple in my kitchen. Combine the granulated sugar with the freshly ground decorticated cardamom. Place it in a jar or airtight container and replenish often. Sprinkle it on Hazelnut Cardamom Matchsticks (page 43) and the Cardamom-Scented Pear and Apple Snacking Cake (opposite) before baking. But because I'm so fond of cardamom, there's no stopping me there. I've been known to sprinkle it over fresh fruit, onto a slice of warm buttered toast, or over a bowl of creamy hot porridge, and I even stir it into tea or coffee.

1 cup (200g) sugar

2 tablespoons freshly ground decorticated cardamom (see page 21)

VARIATION: POACHED QUINCE TOPPING During the short window in the fall when quince is available in Northern California, I replace the apple with poached quince, keeping the chunks of pear as described. If you've seen quince at a farmers' market (or happen to know someone with a quince tree), this is a perfect chance to sample an exquisite and somewhat rare fruit that must be eaten cooked. Like pears, quinces ripen from the inside out. They are similarly grainy in texture and have a tough core, and their astringent flavor means that they have to be simmered and sweetened to be enjoyed. For poaching purposes, it is fine to use very firm fruit, as they will soften in their poaching liquid. It is also fine if they look a little battered and bruised. Quince turn a pretty shade of dusty pink in the poaching liquid as the fruit cooks and softens. This poached quince recipe is a rare instance in this cookbook when whole cardamom pods are called for, which are good for imparting flavor and easy to fish out of the syrup once the fruit is poached.

2 cups (473 g) water, plus more as needed

¾ cup (150 g) sugar

½ cup (170 g) honey

2 teaspoons fresh lemon juice

4 cardamom pods

2 to 3 large quinces (about 500 g total)

In a medium saucepan over medium heat, combine the water, sugar, honey, lemon juice, and cardamom pods and bring to a simmer.

Peel and core the quinces, chop them into ½-inch squares, then immediately add them to the simmering poaching liquid. Cook at a gentle simmer, partially covered, for 1 to 2 hours, checking occasionally for doneness and adding a splash more water if needed. The chunks should be intact and fork-tender and be a pale dusty pink color.

When you are ready to top your snacking cake with the poached quince, strain the chunks. (I suggest reserving the poaching liquid for a delicious addition to a craft cocktail or seltzer water.) Pat the pieces dry and place the drained chunks, together with the pieces of 1 raw pear, in an even layer on top of the cake batter, then sprinkle with the cardamom sugar and bake as directed. You want the chunks of quince to cover the batter in a single layer, and you may have some poached quince left over. If so, lucky you! Poached quince is a tasty seasonal topping for oatmeal or granola, as well as yogurt or ice cream.

WILD BLUEBERRY CARROT CAKE WITH LEMONY CREAM CHEESE FROSTING

In the summer, tiny and intensely flavored blueberries grow wild in parts of Scandinavia. While wild blueberries aren't an easy food to forage in the United States, wild blueberries are available in the frozen aisle at Trader Joe's, adding a burst of welcome tartness to carrot cake. I recommend choosing frozen wild blueberries over giant fresh blueberries, which can be watery and lack the desired tanginess. This cake uses oil instead of butter, so it's extremely moist as well as easy to make. If you'd like, you can do it all by hand without a mixer. You can also bake the cake in a Bundt pan; just remember to adjust the baking time until a toothpick inserted in the center of the cake comes out clean. **MAKES ONE 9-INCH (23 CM) DOUBLE-LAYER CAKE**

Cake

- Butter for greasing the pan
- ½ cup (45 g) walnuts
- 2 cups (256 g) all-purpose flour
- 2 teaspoons baking powder
- 2 teaspoons ground cinnamon
- 1 teaspoon baking soda
- 1 teaspoon kosher salt
- 1 cup (200 g) granulated sugar
- ½ cup (130 g) packed light brown sugar
- 1 cup (220 g) vegetable oil
- 4 eggs
- 4 medium carrots (260 g), grated
- 2 cups (250 g) wild blueberries (frozen is fine, no need to defrost)

→ INGREDIENTS CONTINUED

MAKE THE CAKE

Butter two 9-inch (23 cm) cake pans and line the bottoms with parchment paper. Preheat the oven to 350°F (175°C).

Place the walnuts on a baking tray and toast them in the oven until fragrant, 8 to 10 minutes. Allow them to cool and then coarsely chop them.

In a large bowl, whisk together the flour, baking powder, cinnamon, baking soda, and salt.

In a separate large bowl or in the bowl of a stand mixer fitted with the whisk attachment, whisk together the granulated sugar, brown sugar, oil, and eggs. Add the flour mixture and whisk until just combined. Then add the carrots, blueberries, and walnuts and stir the batter until no lumps remain.

Place the prepared pans on an unlined baking tray and pour in the batter, smoothing it out with a rubber spatula.

Bake for 45 to 50 minutes, rotating the pans halfway through, until the tops and edges are dark golden brown and a toothpick inserted into the center of the cakes comes out clean. Allow the cakes to cool for about 10 minutes before removing them from the pans and placing them on a rack. Cool completely before frosting.

CONTINUED

WILD BLUEBERRY CARROT CAKE WITH LEMONY CREAM CHEESE FROSTING, CONTINUED

Lemony cream cheese frosting

½ cup (113 g) unsalted butter, at room temperature

8 ounces (226 g) cream cheese, at room temperature

1½ to 2 cups (150 to 225 g) powdered sugar

2 tablespoons fresh lemon juice (from ½ to 1 lemon)

1 teaspoon vanilla extract

Pinch of kosher salt

WHILE THE CAKE IS COOLING, MAKE THE FROSTING

In the bowl of a stand mixer fitted with the paddle attachment, beat the butter on medium speed until smooth and creamy, 3 to 4 minutes. Add the cream cheese and beat until well blended, pausing halfway through to scrape the sides and bottom of the bowl with a rubber spatula. Decrease the speed to low and add 1½ cups (150 g) of the powdered sugar, 1 tablespoon of the lemon juice, the vanilla, and the salt. As the sugar is incorporated, increase the speed to medium-high and beat for 3 minutes more. Taste and add the remaining ½ cup (75 g) powdered sugar and 1 tablespoon lemon juice, if needed. You want your frosting to be easy to spread but not too runny.

ASSEMBLE

Using a rubber spatula, spread about ¾ cup (136 g) of the frosting in a thin layer across the surface and out to the edges of one cake, then stack the second cake on top. Continue to frost the rest of the cake, starting with the top and then spreading the frosting down and around the sides. Serve immediately or chill until ready to serve. Store the cake in an airtight container in the refrigerator, where it will stay fresh for up to 3 days. You can also freeze the unfrosted cake layers, wrapped in plastic, then thaw them before frosting the cake.

BROWN SUGAR "FOCACCIA" CAKE

Brunsviger

Brunsviger is a specialty from the isle of Funen, which is the third largest island in Denmark and the birthplace of fairy-tale author Hans Christian Andersen. The bready, pull-apart texture of this dough makes this cake unique, as well as its mixture of warm spices. If you've never baked a yeasted cake before, you will be amazed by how easy it is to make this one, which looks almost exactly like focaccia. After the dough rises in the pan, you create dimples across the surface using your fingertips, then pour a buttery syrup all over it. This syrup pools in the depressions, caramelizing as the cake bakes. In Denmark, brunsviger is something to be enjoyed in the afternoon with a cup of coffee, though in my family we rewarm that a leftover chunk for breakfast, and I can't blame anyone for that! MAKES ONE 9 BY 16-INCH (23 BY 40 CM) SHEET CAKE

Cake

¼ cup (50 g) unsalted butter, cut into small pieces, at room temperature, plus more for greasing

1½ cups (360 g) whole milk

2 tablespoons active dry yeast

2 eggs

¼ cup (50 g) granulated sugar

1½ teaspoons kosher salt

1 teaspoon freshly ground decorticated cardamom (see page 21)

½ teaspoon ground star anise

4½ cups (600 g) all-purpose flour

Topping

1 cup (226 g) unsalted butter

¾ cup (150 g) granulated sugar

¾ cup (160 g) packed light brown sugar

1 tablespoon malt syrup (see page 24)

MAKE THE CAKE

Generously butter a 13 by 18-inch (33 by 46 cm) baking tray.

In a small saucepan over medium heat, heat the milk to about 98°F (36°C), so it feels just slightly warm to the touch.

In the bowl of a stand mixer fitted with the dough hook attachment, combine the yeast, eggs, sugar, salt, cardamom, star anise, and 2 cups (256 g) of the flour and mix on low. With the mixer running, slowly pour in the warm milk and mix until a dough is formed. Scrape the sides and bottom of the bowl with a rubber spatula. Add the remaining 2½ cups (344 g) of flour and mix until it is incorporated, then add the butter. Mix the dough on medium speed until it is smooth and elastic, about 6 minutes.

Cover the bowl with a kitchen towel and let the dough rest for 10 minutes. Transfer the dough to the prepared baking tray and, using your hands, push the dough out into an even slab, reaching into the corners of the baking tray.

Cover the baking tray with a towel and allow the dough to rest and rise until it is fluffy and doubled in thickness, about 1 hour.

MEANWHILE, PREPARE THE TOPPING

In a small saucepan over low heat, melt the butter, granulated sugar, brown sugar, and malt syrup, stirring to combine. Remove from the heat and allow the mixture cool to room temperature while the dough proofs.

CONTINUED

Once the dough is ready, stir the sugar-butter mixture and then pour it evenly over the dough. Using your fingertips, make indentations every half inch or so across the dough, creating small pools for the topping to flow into.

Cover the dough with plastic wrap and let it proof for 30 minutes more. About halfway through, preheat the oven to 375°F (190°C).

Bake for 25 to 30 minutes, until the top has turned a dark bronze and the cake is baked through. Cut it into 2-inch (5 cm) squares. This cake is most delicious eaten warm from the oven on the day it is baked. Or you can store it in an airtight container for up to 3 days; just freshen it up in a 350°F (175°C) oven for 7 to 9 minutes before eating.

BLACKBERRY TOSCA CAKE

Toscakaka med Björnbär

A Swedish fika favorite, tosca cakes are composed of a layer of moist cake tucked beneath a caramelized almond topping. No one knows for sure where the cake got its name, but one theory is that it is connected to the Scandinavian premiere of Puccini's opera *Tosca*. This cake is typically made without the addition of fresh fruit, but years ago at Kantine we happened to buy a surplus load of organic fresh blackberries and experimented by adding them to different recipes. This tweak on a classic Swedish cake was a winner. Be sure to read through the entire recipe before getting started, as there is an important time factor regarding the making of the topping. MAKES ONE 9-INCH (23 CM) CAKE

Cake

½ cup plus 1 tablespoon (127 g) unsalted butter, plus more for greasing

1 egg, at room temperature

¾ cup (150 g) sugar

½ cup (120 g) whole milk, lukewarm

1 teaspoon vanilla extract

1¼ cups (160 g) all-purpose flour

1 teaspoon baking powder

½ teaspoon kosher salt

1½ cups (192 g) blackberries (fresh or frozen)

Topping

7 tablespoons (100 g) unsalted butter, cut into small pieces

¾ cup (75 g) sliced almonds

½ cup (100 g) sugar

2 tablespoons all-purpose flour

2 tablespoons whole milk

Pinch of kosher salt

MAKE THE CAKE

Butter a 9-inch (23 cm) cake pan with a removable bottom, line the bottom with parchment paper, and butter the parchment paper. Line a 13 by 18-inch (33 by 46 cm) baking tray with parchment paper or a silicone baking mat. Place the cake pan in the center of the baking tray to prevent any spills from scorching the bottom of the oven; set aside. Preheat the oven to 350°F (175°C).

In a small saucepan over medium-high heat, melt the butter and then set it aside to cool.

In the bowl of a stand mixer fitted with the whisk attachment, beat the egg on high for about 2 minutes, until it looks fluffy and has doubled in volume. Gradually add the sugar and mix until it turns a pale yellow, about 3 minutes more. Decrease the speed to low and add the cooled melted butter, the milk, and the vanilla and beat for 1 minute. Switch to the paddle attachment.

In a large bowl, whisk together the flour, baking powder, and salt. Add the flour mixture to the butter mixture and mix on low until the batter is lump-free. Finish by stirring with a rubber spatula. The batter should have a lovely sheen and be fairly liquid.

Pour the batter into the prepared pan, smoothing it out with the spatula. Distribute the blackberries evenly in a single layer across the surface of the batter. It's okay if they sink. Once the cake has baked for 30 minutes, keep it baking in the oven, but begin to make the topping.

CONTINUED

MAKE THE TOPPING

In a medium saucepan over medium-high heat, combine the butter, almonds, sugar, flour, milk, and salt and cook, stirring as the butter melts, until a few bubbles form at the edge of the pan. Decrease the heat to medium-low and continue to cook, stirring nonstop, for 3 minutes more. When the mixture has thickened so that your spatula leaves a track as you stir, remove the pan from the heat.

TOP THE CAKE

Carefully remove the cake from the oven, leaving the oven on, and scatter spoonfuls of the topping onto the cake. Do this gently (the cake will still be fragile). Use an offset spatula or knife to spread the topping evenly across the surface and out to the edges of the cake. Bake for 15 to 20 minutes more, until the caramel on top of the cake looks dark and is bubbling. Allow the cake to cool completely before removing it from the pan. This cake is best enjoyed on the day it is baked. Or you can store it in an airtight container in the refrigerator for up to 3 days.

BUDAPEST ROLL

Budapestrulle

Made of hazelnut meringue rolled around whipped cream and tangerine segments, this elegant cake was the creation of a Swedish pastry chef in the 1950s and has no roots in Budapest at all! It makes a terrific dessert choice in the winter when citrus is one of the only fresh fruits in season. But it would be equally delicious in the summer made with sliced apricots, peaches, or raspberries. The batter is piped into strips before baking, which minimizes cracking when you fill and roll it up. While this technique might sound complicated, once you get the hang of using a piping bag, it's not difficult. This cake can be made ahead of time and refrigerated for one day. It definitely looks fancy enough to form the pièce de résistance as part of a celebratory meal.

MAKES 1 ROLL CAKE THAT SERVES 8 TO 10

Butter for greasing

1½ cups (200 g) hazelnuts

1 tablespoon cornstarch

6 egg whites

Pinch of kosher salt

½ cup (100 g) granulated sugar

2 cups (453 g) heavy cream

½ cup (50 g) powdered sugar, plus more for garnish

12 to 15 tangerines (about 1.2 kg total), peeled, seeds and pith removed

To finish

1 ounce (28 g) 63% (or higher) bittersweet chocolate

Butter a 10 by 15-inch (25 by 38 cm) jelly roll pan and line the bottom with parchment paper. (If your pan is a slightly different size, that's okay; you will pipe the meringue in strips until you run out of batter.) Preheat the oven to 400°F (200°C).

In a food processor, pulse the hazelnuts to a coarse sand, being careful not to turn them into nut butter. In a medium bowl, stir together the ground hazelnuts and the cornstarch.

In the bowl of a stand mixer fitted with the whisk attachment, beat the egg whites and salt on medium until they are soft and foamy and have doubled in volume. Add the granulated sugar gradually, one spoonful at a time, and beat on high until stiff peaks form, 3 to 5 minutes.

Using a rubber spatula, fold the hazelnut mixture into the egg whites, being careful to deflate the egg whites as little as possible. Use the spatula to transfer the meringue batter into a piping bag fitted with a plain tip.

Pipe the batter in straight lines running parallel to the short side of the prepared pan, with each line touching the next, moving from one end of the pan toward the other. Don't worry about ridges. They should resemble long ladyfingers, laid side by side. Try not to let the batter touch any of the pan edges (leave a border of about 1 inch/2.5 cm) so that the meringue doesn't stick to the metal. Stop piping when you run out of meringue (for reference, I end up with about a 10 by 11-inch/25 by 27 cm rectangle).

CONTINUED

Bake the meringue layer for 8 to 9 minutes, until the top is fairly evenly browned. Then decrease the temperature to 350°F (175°C) and continue baking for 10 minutes more, until the meringue is firm to the touch. While the meringue is baking, line another baking tray with parchment paper.

Immediately after removing the meringue from the oven, carefully invert the meringue onto the prepared baking tray. Peel off the parchment paper backing. Score a line ½ inch (1 cm) in from the short edge of the meringue, fold the scored end in, and roll up the meringue (wrapping it around the parchment paper as you roll). This will allow it to keep its rolled shape while preventing it from breaking later when you add the whipped cream and fruit. Let the roll cool completely, about 30 minutes.

Meanwhile, in the bowl of a stand mixer fitted with the whisk attachment, whip the cream and powdered sugar on medium-high speed until soft peaks form, 3 to 4 minutes. Be careful not to overwhip the cream (see page 37).

Carefully unroll the cake and discard the parchment paper. Spread a layer of the whipped cream over the entire inside of the roll, reserving about 1 cup. Evenly disperse the tangerine segments across the surface of the whipped cream, reserving a handful for decorating the cake, and carefully roll up the cake again (without the parchment paper, this time).

Carefully transfer the roll to a serving platter and chill for at least 1 hour in the refrigerator or until ready to serve. Right before serving, sift powdered sugar over the top of the roll and decorate with small dollops of the remaining whipped cream and the reserved tangerine segments. With a Microplane or nutmeg grater, grate the chocolate directly over the roulade immediately before serving. Store leftover cake in an airtight container in the refrigerator for up to 2 days.

SUMMER STRAWBERRY TART WITH CUSTARD AND CHOCOLATE

Jordbærtærte

In Denmark, strawberry season is so short and sweet—emphasis on sweet—that people eat almost nothing else as long as they're available. Danish strawberries are on the small side, red through and through, and as soft and juicy as a perfect peach. In late July when they're truly at their peak, people often eat them straight from the field or out of the small crates in which they are sold. But they also love to bake with them, very often featuring them fresh and pure in tarts.

There are as many versions of strawberry tarts in Denmark as there are recipes for pumpkin pie at Thanksgiving in America. But if you ask me, a classic Danish strawberry tart should include layers of vanilla pastry cream, almond filling, dark chocolate, and heaps of ruby-red strawberries. This flavor combination always reminds me of a great éclair combined with chocolate-dipped strawberries. Because it has four components, this tart takes more time and effort to assemble than some of the other recipes in this chapter. But it's worth the work if you have a worthy occasion (which could just be celebrating strawberry season itself!). To make this tart, use a 9½-inch (24 cm) fluted tart pan with a removable bottom. **MAKES ONE 9½-INCH (24 CM) TART THAT SERVES 8 TO 10**

Crust

1½ cups (192 g) all-purpose flour, plus more for dusting

7 tablespoons (98 g) unsalted butter, cold, cut into small pieces

Pinch of kosher salt

½ cup (61 g) powdered sugar

2 egg yolks

1 to 2 teaspoons ice water

1 pound (455 g) dried beans, for blind baking (see page 23)

→ INGREDIENTS CONTINUED

MAKE THE CRUST

In the bowl of a stand mixer fitted with the paddle attachment, beat the flour, butter, and salt on low until the butter forms pea-size pieces. Add the powdered sugar and egg yolks and increase the speed to medium, mixing the dough for 1 minute more. Add the ice water, 1 teaspoon at a time, mixing just until the dough comes together. Turn out the dough onto a work surface and finish forming it by hand until it becomes a smooth and glossy ball. Wrap the dough in parchment paper or plastic wrap and chill for at least 30 minutes in the refrigerator.

WHILE THE DOUGH CHILLS, MAKE THE ALMOND FILLING

In the bowl of a stand mixer fitted with the whisk attachment, beat the almond paste, powdered sugar, and butter on low. You may want to drape a dish towel around the mouth of the mixing bowl at first in order to keep the powdered sugar contained. Once the powdered sugar has been incorporated, increase the speed to medium and mix until it looks smooth and creamy. Scrape the sides and bottom of the bowl with a rubber spatula. Add the flour and salt and mix again on low until the

SUMMER STRAWBERRY TART WITH CUSTARD AND CHOCOLATE, CONTINUED

Almond filling

⅓ cup plus 2 tablespoons (100 g) almond paste (see page 21)

¾ cup (100 g) powdered sugar

5 tablespoons (75 g) unsalted butter, at room temperature

2 tablespoons all-purpose flour

Pinch of kosher salt

2 eggs

3 ounces (75 g) 63% (or higher) bittersweet chocolate, finely chopped

Pastry cream

1 cup (240 g) whole milk

1 vanilla bean, split lengthwise

2 egg yolks

3 tablespoons granulated sugar

1 tablespoon cornstarch

1 pound (456 g) strawberries, hulled and halved (see Note)

Glaze

2 tablespoons apricot jam

2 tablespoons water

flour is incorporated. Add the eggs, one at a time, continuing to mix between additions. The filling should have the consistency of a soft cream cheese frosting. Set the filling aside while you roll out your crust.

Preheat the oven to 350°F (175°C).

Lightly dust a work surface with flour and roll the chilled dough into a 12-inch (30 cm) circle using the "air hockey" method (see page 36). To transfer the dough to the tart pan, gently curl it around your rolling pin. This makes the dough easier to carry to the pan without it breaking. Uncurl it from the rolling pin directly over the pan and carefully press it down into the bottom and against the sides of the pan. Use your fingertip or the edge of a knife to trim any excess overhang.

To blind bake the crust, place a generous sheet of parchment paper over the dough and then fill the tart shell with the dried beans, heaped on top of the parchment paper. Place the tart pan on a baking tray and bake for 20 minutes, until the top edges of the crust are golden. Remove the tart pan from the oven, leaving the oven on, and remove the parchment paper and beans.

Pour the almond filling into the blind-baked tart shell, using a mini offset spatula or the back of a spoon to spread it evenly across the surface. Bake the tart for about 25 minutes, until the almond layer looks and feels set in the center.

Place the tart on a rack and sprinkle the chocolate over the top, where it should melt within minutes. Once it has melted, use an offset spatula to spread the chocolate evenly across the entire surface, avoiding the crust, and allow the tart to cool completely in the pan.

WHILE THE TART COOLS, MAKE THE PASTRY CREAM

Add the milk to a small saucepan. Scrape the seeds from the vanilla bean into the milk, then add the scraped pod. Bring the mixture to a simmer over low heat, turning the heat off as soon as you see bubbles forming at the edge of the pan. Fish out and discard the vanilla pod.

In a small bowl, whisk the egg yolks, granulated sugar, and cornstarch to a smooth and uniform paste.

Add about ½ (120 g) cup of the scalded milk to the egg mixture and whisk together, then add this back to the pan with the rest of the milk. Bring to a gentle simmer over medium-low heat and cook, whisking continuously, for 2 to 3 minutes, until a thick pasty cream forms. Transfer the custard to a small bowl. Place a piece of plastic wrap directly onto the surface of the pastry cream and chill it for at least 30 minutes in the refrigerator.

ASSEMBLE

Remove the plastic wrap from the chilled pastry cream (see Note). Using a mini offset spatula, spread the pastry cream over the melted chocolate layer in the tart shell. Arrange the strawberries cut side down in a circular pattern over the top, with the stem ends pointing out toward the crust. The strawberries should touch but not overlap (see Note).

MAKE THE GLAZE

In a small saucepan over medium-high heat, combine the apricot jam and water, whisking until it comes to a simmer. Remove the pan from the stove and let the glaze cool for a few minutes.

With a pastry brush, lightly brush the glaze over each of the strawberries, which will give the tart a fresh and glossy finish and keep the fruit from drying out.

Serve immediately or chill in the refrigerator until ready to serve. This tart is best eaten on the day it is made.

NOTE Larger strawberries look better cut, but if you are lucky enough to get your hands on tiny ones or even wild strawberries, they would be pretty hulled but left whole, and heaped onto the tart.

ROASTED NUT AND CARAMEL TART

Kolapaj med Nötter

I was first introduced to kolapaj by a delightful couple named Jeannette and Roland, who are regulars at Kantine. They first came into Kantine shortly after a trip to Scandinavia, having fallen in love with the culture and food and wanting more of it. They told me about a nut and caramel tart that they'd encountered at a restaurant in Sweden. They loved it so much that they had one shipped from that Swedish restaurant all the way to San Francisco! Hearing that, I felt compelled to research the recipe and try baking one. I learned that kolapaj (which translates to "caramel pie") can be made with or without nuts. Wanting to get as close as possible to the one about which Jeanette and Roland raved, I went for the nut-filled version. One thing that sets this apart from pecan pie—aside from the sweetened tart crust—is the inclusion of a variety of nuts. I use equal parts walnuts, hazelnuts, cashews, pistachios, and macadamia nuts. Feel free to combine whatever raw unsalted nuts you think would taste good here. MAKES ONE 9½-INCH (24 CM) TART THAT SERVES 8 TO 10

Crust

1 crust from Strawberry Summer Tart (page 91)

All-purpose flour for dusting

1 pound (455 g) dried beans, for blind baking (see page 23)

Caramel filling

3 eggs

¾ cup (150 g) sugar

½ cup (170 g) light corn syrup

2 teaspoons vanilla extract

¼ cup (85 g) heavy cream

6 tablespoons (98 g) unsalted butter, melted

½ teaspoon kosher salt

3 cups (340 g) mixed nuts, any variety

Unsweetened whipped cream or crème fraîche for serving

MAKE THE CRUST

Follow the directions for making the crust on page 91 to the point where the dough is wrapped and chilled for 30 minutes.

Once you are ready to roll out your crust, preheat the oven to 350°F (175°C).

Lightly dust a work surface with flour and roll the chilled dough into a 12-inch (30 cm) circle, using the "air hockey" method (see page 36). To transfer the dough to the tart pan, gently curl it around your rolling pin. This makes the dough easier to carry to the pan without it breaking. Uncurl it from the rolling pin directly over the pan and carefully press it down into the bottom and against the sides of the pan. Use your fingertip or the edge of a knife to trim any excess overhang.

To blind bake the crust, place a generous sheet of parchment paper over the dough and then fill the tart shell with the dried beans, heaped on top of the parchment paper. Place the tart pan on a baking tray and bake for 20 minutes, until the top edges of the crust are golden.

WHILE THE CRUST IS BAKING, MAKE THE CARAMEL FILLING

In the bowl of a stand mixer fitted with the whisk attachment, beat the eggs, sugar, and corn syrup on medium until frothy, 1 to 2 minutes. Add the vanilla, cream, butter, and salt and mix until incorporated.

CONTINUED

Remove the crust from the oven, leaving the oven on. Remove the parchment paper and beans.

Place the tart on an unlined baking tray. Spread the nuts over the crust and pour the caramel over the nuts. It should come all the way to the top of the crust.

Bake for 40 to 50 minutes, until the caramel on top is a dark golden brown and the edges of the crust are a lighter brown. Allow the kolapaj to cool completely before cutting it into slices. Serve with unsweetened whipped cream to complement the caramel's sweetness. This tart is best enjoyed on the day it is baked. Or you can store it in an airtight container in the refrigerator for up to 2 days.

CAKE PERSON

Kageperson

If you ask me, no Danish child's birthday party would be complete without a "cake person." Choux pastry gets piped into the form of a person that is meant to represent the birthday kid, decorated in royal icing stuck with gobs of candy. If your piping is messy, don't worry about it. Nobody will notice once the pastry gets buried under all that candy. Both kids and adults love to see this cake brought out during a party. It's also a fun project to tackle with a kid, who can choose what candy to use and where to put it. The cake person's head always gets the most, usually in the form of licorice ropes. Danes love black licorice and tend to use it heavily to decorate this dessert, but feel free to substitute the candies of your choice if licorice isn't your thing. Make it as colorful and detailed as you can, and don't be afraid if the effect is a little disturbing. It's part of the fun! MAKES 1 CAKE PERSON

Choux pastry

1 cup (240 g) whole milk

1 cup (237 g) water

½ cup (113 g) unsalted butter

1 tablespoon (10 g) granulated sugar

½ teaspoon kosher salt

1¼ cups (160 g) all-purpose flour

4 eggs

Royal icing

1 cup (100 g) powdered sugar

1 to 3 tablespoons water

To finish

About 2 cups of assorted candy, including black and red licorice, gummy candies, hard candies, or whatever other types of candy you like, plus candy hair

Line a 13 by 18-inch (33 by 46 cm) baking tray with parchment paper. Using a pencil, draw a gingerbread man–shaped figure on the parchment paper. The figure should fill most of the paper. Turn the paper over so that the pencil lead doesn't transfer to the dough (you should still be able to clearly see the outline of the shape). Set aside.

MAKE THE CHOUX PASTRY

In a large saucepan over medium heat, combine the milk, water, butter, granulated sugar, and salt. Bring the mixture to a boil, then remove from the heat.

Add the flour and return the pan to the stove over medium-high heat. Whisk continuously for 3 to 4 minutes while the mixture cooks, until it congeals to a lump and a skin forms at the bottom of the pot.

Transfer the mixture to the bowl of a stand mixer fitted with the paddle attachment. Mix on medium until the steam dissipates. Once the dough is no longer steaming, add the eggs one at a time while mixing. It should form a wet, supple, and glossy dough.

Preheat the oven to 400°F (200°C).

To pipe your cake person, use a rubber spatula to transfer the dough to a piping bag fitted with a medium plain tip (see page 22). Holding your piping bag upright with the tip down, gently squeeze out the dough while following the outline of the person on the prepared parchment paper. Once you've outlined the form, fill it in with the rest of the dough. You don't need to be extremely precise. You can use a moistened fingertip to

smooth out the ridges if you'd like, but since you will be decorating this figure with icing and candy, it doesn't matter if it's a little rough.

Bake for 35 to 40 minutes, until the dough has expanded and is dark golden in color.

WHILE THE CAKE IS BAKING, MAKE THE ICING

In a small bowl, whisk together the powdered sugar and 1 tablespoon of the water. Add more water, 1 tablespoon at a time, until it has the consistency of loose honey.

Allow the Cake Person to cool completely. Use a small offset spatula to spread the icing over the surface of the cake person and then stick your candy to the icing. Let it cool completely so that the candy is glued in place and then serve! I've heard that many people begin to serve by first cutting off the person's head! And I've also seen a version of a cake person where fresh fruit (berries, orange segments, grapes, kiwi slices) were used to decorate the cake instead of candy. To each their own, I say! This cake is best eaten on the day it is made.

ROYAL PARTY CAKE

Kongelig Kage

The royal party cake is a magnificent study in textural contrasts. Two layers of soft vanilla cake are topped with crunchy walnuts and a chewy layer of meringue, then covered with a cloud of whipped cream. The whole thing is then scattered with fresh berries that have been tossed with elderberry syrup. While I sometimes find meringue to be too sweet, I love it in this cake, especially because I don't add sugar to the whipped cream, which is mixed with sour cream, a tangy counterpoint to the sweet meringue. Bake this cake for a special occasion or make any occasion special by baking this cake! It truly is a party in and of itself. At the height of summer, I recommend combining a few different berries to garnish the cake. Raspberries and red currants provide a distinctly Scandinavian taste, but any juicy, sweet fruit will do. In the winter you could make this cake with stewed fruits like apple or pear. **MAKES ONE 9-INCH (23 CM) DOUBLE-LAYER CAKE THAT SERVES 8 TO 10**

Cake

¾ cup (170 g) unsalted butter, at room temperature, plus more for greasing

¾ cup (150 g) sugar

4 egg yolks, at room temperature

1 teaspoon vanilla extract

⅓ cup (70 g) whole milk

1 cup plus 1 tablespoon (150 g) all-purpose flour

2 teaspoons baking powder

¼ teaspoon kosher salt

4 ounces (113 g) walnuts, coarsely chopped

→ INGREDIENTS CONTINUED

MAKE THE CAKE

Generously butter two 9-inch (23 cm) cake pans with removable bottoms, line the bottoms with parchment paper, and butter the parchment paper. This cake tends to stick, so be liberal with the butter. Preheat the oven to 350°F (175°C).

In the bowl of a stand mixer fitted with the paddle attachment, beat the butter and sugar on medium until soft and creamy, pausing halfway through to scrape the sides and bottom of the bowl with a rubber spatula, 2 to 3 minutes. Add the egg yolks, one at a time, mixing until each is well incorporated. Then add the vanilla and milk, mixing to combine.

In a small bowl, whisk together the flour, baking powder, and salt. Add the flour mixture to the butter mixture and mix on low until the batter is smooth.

Divide the batter evenly between the prepared pans, smoothing it out with a rubber spatula. Sprinkle the nuts evenly over the top of each cake. (If you are using a scale to weigh your ingredients, use about 55 g of walnuts per pan.) Don't be alarmed if that doesn't look like a lot of batter. You will be adding the meringue directly on top, which will puff up in the oven.

MAKE THE MERINGUE

Thoroughly wash and dry your mixer bowl. Using the whisk attachment, beat the egg whites and salt on high until soft peaks form. With the mixer running, slowly add the sugar and beat until stiff and glossy, about 5 minutes.

CONTINUED

Meringue layer

4 egg whites, at room temperature

Pinch of kosher salt

1 cup (200 g) sugar

Whipped cream topping

1½ cups (360 g) whipping cream

½ cup (120 g) sour cream

Berries

1 cup (118 g) fresh red currants, or other flavorful fresh berry

2 cups (250 g) fresh raspberries

3 tablespoons elderflower syrup (see Note)

Divide the meringue between the pans, directly over the cake batter and nuts, and spread it so that it covers the surface but stops short of touching the edges of the pans. Meringue is quite sticky, and not pushing it to the edges of the pan will make it easier to remove the baked cakes. The meringue layers don't need to be perfectly smooth as they will be covered in whipped cream.

Place the two pans on an unlined baking tray. Bake for 45 to 50 minutes, until the meringue is light brown. After removing the cakes from the oven, put them on a rack to cool to room temperature before unmolding. Line a 13 by 18-inch (33 by 46 cm) baking tray with parchment paper. To unmold each cake, run a knife around the edge of the pan. Carefully invert the cake onto a plate and peel off the parchment paper. Flip the cake back onto its bottom and transfer to the parchment-lined baking tray. Set aside until ready to use. The meringue-topped cakes can be baked 1 day in advance and assembled before serving.

ONCE THE CAKES HAVE COOLED, MAKE THE TOPPING

In the bowl of a stand mixer fitted with the whisk attachment or in a large bowl with a handheld mixer, whip the cream on medium until soft peaks form (see page 37). Whisk in the sour cream until just incorporated and set aside.

PREPARE THE BERRIES

Remove the delicate stems from all but a few clusters of red currants, reserving those to garnish the top of the cake. Place the stemmed red currants and the raspberries in a large bowl. Pour the elderberry syrup over them and stir them gently so that the fruit is well coated in syrup. This will add a Scandinavian floral note to the berries and bring out their juices.

Place one cake layer on a serving platter, meringue facing up, and top with half of the whipped topping and half of the elderflower-soaked berries and currants. Stack the second layer on top, then spread the top with the remaining whipped topping. Top with the rest of the berries, finishing with the reserved red currants still attached to their stems. This cake is best eaten on the day it is assembled.

NOTE Elderberry syrup is available online and through World Market. I like the Darbo brand.

BUTTERMILK "SOUP" WITH CARDAMOM RUSKS

Koldskål med Kammerjunker

This is a quintessential Danish Midsummer dish, sometimes even eaten for dinner on the hottest nights when no one feels like cooking in a sweltering kitchen. (And maybe people are tired from staying up dancing and partying in the endless daylight as well!) The cold "soup" is made of buttermilk thickened with whipped egg yolks and sugar and chilled. Fresh strawberries get sliced into each bowl; then it is topped off with cardamom rusks—a hard cookie that gets baked twice like biscotti. They hold up well to extreme dunking, remaining crunchy even after they soak in the buttermilk soup. If this is a dessert "soup," imagine the cookies are your soup croutons! The big debate is to crumble them or to leave them whole? I'm a crumbler, myself. Ideally, make both the cardamom rusks and the soup a day before you want to enjoy the dish. The rusks get crunchier overnight, and chilling the soup overnight amplifies the vanilla flavor.

MAKES 4 TO 6 SERVINGS

Cardamom rusks

- ¼ cup (56 g) unsalted butter, melted
- ¼ cup plus 1 tablespoon (65 g) sugar
- 2 tablespoons whole milk
- 2 eggs
- 2 cups (256 g) all-purpose flour, plus more for dusting
- ¾ teaspoon baking powder
- ¼ teaspoon kosher salt
- ½ teaspoon freshly ground decorticated cardamom (see page 21)

Buttermilk "soup"

- 3 egg yolks
- ½ cup (100 g) sugar
- 1 vanilla bean, split lengthwise
- 4 cups (1 L) buttermilk
- 1 tablespoon fresh lemon juice

→ INGREDIENTS CONTINUED

MAKE THE CARDAMOM RUSKS

Line a 13 by 18-inch (33 by 46 cm) baking tray with parchment paper and preheat the oven to 325°F (165°C).

In the bowl of a stand mixer fitted with the whisk attachment, beat the butter and sugar on medium until the sugar has dissolved. Add the milk and eggs and beat until well incorporated.

In a large bowl, whisk together the flour, baking powder, salt, and cardamom. Switch to the paddle attachment. Add the flour mixture to the butter mixture and mix on low for 1 to 2 minutes, until it forms a shaggy dough. Be careful not to overmix. Turn the dough out onto a work surface and knead by hand until the dough is smooth.

Divide the dough into four equal portions. Lightly dust a work surface with flour and then roll each portion into a log with a 1-inch (2.5 cm) diameter. Place four logs side by side on the prepared baking tray. Bake for about 15 minutes, rotating the baking trays front to back halfway through, until pale brown.

Remove the baking tray from the oven and decrease the temperature to 200°F (95°C). Allow the logs to cool until you are able to handle them, then cut each log into about twenty cookies at ½-inch (1 cm) intervals. Or to get a rustic, jagged edge, use the tines of a fork to pry off the slices; some say the nooks and crannies sop up more soup. Arrange them on the same baking tray and bake for an additional

30 to 40 minutes, rotating the baking tray halfway through, until they are golden and dried out. (You can also make the rusks well ahead of time, as they stay crunchy for up to 2 weeks in an airtight container.)

To finish

3 to 4 cups (498 g to 664 g) fresh ripe strawberries, hulled and quartered

WHILE THE RUSKS ARE BAKING, MAKE THE BUTTERMILK "SOUP"

In the bowl of a stand mixer fitted with the whisk attachment, beat the egg yolks and sugar until thick and doubled in volume, 3 to 4 minutes. Scrape the seeds from the vanilla bean into the egg mixture and combine. Gradually add the buttermilk on low speed, followed by the lemon juice.

Transfer the soup to an airtight container or cover with plastic wrap and chill for at least 2 hours (or ideally overnight) in the refrigerator.

Serve the soup alongside a serving bowl of the strawberries and cardamom rusks, so that people can help themselves to the toppings. Encourage them to add more midway through eating their bowls, ensuring that each bite is "just right." Store the soup in an airtight container in the refrigerator, where it will stay fresh for up to 4 days.

A BIT ABOUT MIDSUMMER

Midsummer, the summer solstice and longest day of the year, falls on June 21. In some northern parts of Scandinavia, the sun never sets on that day.

Summers in Scandinavia are straight out of a fairy tale. I've been woken many times in the middle of the night by the chirping of the birds. City dwellers bike to the nearest body of water to sun and swim all day and much of the night. Many caravan from one multiday outdoor music festival to another, sleeping in tents and subsisting on beer.

For Midsummer, Swedes dance around the maypole, sing songs, and wear flower wreaths on their heads. In Denmark and Norway, Midsummer and Saint John's Eve are combined into one day of festivities on June 23, and it's generally a calmer affair. Typically, there's a lot of grilled food, rosy red strawberries, and speeches by a bonfire. The food eaten on Midsummer is not fancy. Groups gather to cook outside in the lingering daylight. A Danish tradition is to wind raw pizza dough around a thick stick that gets held over the fire, so the dough bakes into a curlicue shape when it's peeled off the stick and is enjoyed with ketchup and mustard.

The middle of the summer is also when Scandinavian berries are at their prime, bright and juicy and sweeter than candy, taking center stage in any number of special desserts. Bakers seize the opportunity to create spectacular Midsummer confections featuring the region's delicate and perfect strawberries. Should you wish to throw your own Midsummer dinner party, I suggest making either Royal Party Cake (page 100) or Buttermilk "Soup" with Cardamom Rusks (page 103). Both epitomize beautiful Scandinavian summer nights.

LET'S FIKA!

In Sweden, fika, or the custom of taking a regular coffee break, dates back to the nineteenth century, which was one of the five times in Swedish history when drinking coffee was illegal, as those in charge deemed the coffee bean to be a poison and too "foreign." Coffee lovers sidestepped this law, scrambling the letters for *kaffi* into *fika* and making this their code word for secret gatherings at which they drank the forbidden beverage. Then as now, sweet treats, known as fikabröd, are a must. And when people want to get together for coffee and a treat, they'll say, "Let's fika!"

In the Swedish workplace, fika often happens around ten o'clock and again at three in the afternoon. Add in a lunch break and you've got a day punctuated by opportunities for sweet buns and cakes. Don't you love a culture that makes enjoying pastries such a priority? It's not limited to workdays either. You can also suggest meeting a friend or potential date for fika. Among the most popular fikabröd are kanelbullar (Cinnamon Knots, page 113) and teboller med chokolade (Dark Chocolate Tea Buns, page 111).

Danes also try to carve out time each day to relax and enjoy a cup of coffee with coworkers, often over freshly baked cookies, a slice of cake, or a danish. As you might guess, danishes are the pride of Denmark. Unlike Swedish cinnamon knots, which are made of yeasted brioche dough, the flaky danish is made of a laminated pastry dough called danish dough—logical, huh? What's confusing is that Danes call these flaky pastries wienerbrød, meaning "the bread from Wien" (or Vienna). As with all laminated dough, danish dough is made by wrapping dough around a slab of butter, rolling them out together, folding the dough, and then chilling it. The process is repeated several times, producing a dough containing ultra-thin layers of butter that melts during baking, leaving air pockets that create the flakiness and light texture of the pastry. It's similar to croissant dough, but not entirely the same.

Our sweet and savory danishes at Kantine are among the most popular bakery items, and they're also one of my very favorite things in the world to eat. So, when I decided to write a Scandinavian baking cookbook, I faced a dilemma. On the one hand, I wanted the recipes to be as fuss-free as possible and accessible to the home baker, and unfortunately making your own danish dough isn't the easiest process. But I also can't imagine a Scandinavian cookbook (or life) minus these emblematic danishes—nothing is better than a danish made from scratch that has just come out of the oven. So, I decided to split this collection of pastry recipes in half. The first section of recipes in this chapter yields an assortment of showstopping pastries made with a brioche dough that is straightforward to make in a stand mixer. The second section teaches home cooks how to make laminated dough and offers my favorite danish recipes. These recipes are admittedly more time-consuming and slightly more complex than the ones in the first section of the chapter, but they will teach you new skills as a baker.

Also, while working on this book, I came up with a process for lamination that is relatively easy to do at home, producing bakery-quality flaky layers. The truth is, laminating dough isn't really difficult so much as it requires precision in rolling the dough out and time set aside to chill the dough repeatedly. Luckily, after you've tried this process once, subsequent batches will make a lot more sense and the results will reflect that! But any of these pastries are sure to be the hit of a brunch or party, wowing guests who won't be able to believe that you made them from scratch. Once you learn these dough recipes and shaping techniques, you can get creative with your fillings, taking advantage of whatever is in season to concoct your own versions of Scandinavian classics.

MASTER RECIPE: SOFT BUN DOUGH/BLØDE BOLLER

This basic bun dough recipe is a great starting place for someone who wants to delve into making yeasted pastries like Dark Chocolate Tea Buns (opposite) and Cinnamon Knots (page 113). The recipe requires first making a tangzhong, a technique originally from Japan that is used to make supermoist milk bread. The method was spread across Asia by Taiwanese cookbook author Yvonne Chen and then popularized in the Western world after cookbook author Christine Ho wrote about it in English.

To make a tangzhong, you cook a small portion of milk and flour together before adding it to the remaining dough ingredients. This step allows more hydration to be incorporated into the dough, resulting in bread that stays moist, tender, and fresh much longer. While the technique is not traditional to Scandinavian baking, many modern bakeries in Copenhagen and elsewhere have started incorporating it into traditional recipes, as I do here, for superior results.

Higher hydration levels make this bun dough quite sticky, which is why I strongly recommend making it the night before baking and refrigerating it overnight. This gives it a chance to firm up a little, making it easier to work with. **MAKES 1 BATCH BUN DOUGH**

Tangzhong

3 tablespoons all-purpose flour

½ cup (120 g) whole milk

Dough

½ cup (113 g) unsalted butter, cut into 1-inch (2.5 cm) pieces, at room temperature, plus more for greasing

1½ cups (360 g) whole milk

4½ cups (576 g) all-purpose flour

2½ teaspoons kosher salt

1 egg

1 tablespoon active dry yeast

⅓ cup (66 g) sugar

MAKE THE TANGZHONG

In a small saucepan, whisk the flour and milk so that there are no lumps. Cook over medium heat, whisking constantly, until the mixture becomes elastic, like the consistency of thick glue, about 1 minute. Transfer the mixture to the bowl of a stand mixer and let it cool completely, about 10 minutes.

MAKE THE DOUGH

Butter a medium bowl.

To the mixer bowl holding the cooled tangzhong, add the milk, flour, salt, egg, and yeast. With the dough hook attachment, mix on low until all the ingredients are combined, pausing to scrape the sides and bottom of the bowl with a rubber spatula. Increase the speed to medium and mix for 4 minutes more. Decrease the speed to low and sprinkle in the sugar, 1 tablespoon at a time. Gradually add the butter, one or two pieces at a time, waiting between each addition for them to be incorporated into the dough, then mix for 4 minutes more. The butter should be completely absorbed into a glossy and stretchy dough that is beginning to come off the sides of the bowl.

Transfer the dough to the prepared bowl. Cover it with a kitchen towel or plastic wrap and chill it overnight (up to 12 hours) in the refrigerator or let it rest and rise at room temperature for 2 hours, until you are ready to shape it.

DARK CHOCOLATE TEA BUNS

Teboller med Chokolade

In Scandinavia, the standard tea bun is soft and lightly sweet with a smidge of ground cardamom or cinnamon. Sometimes raisins are added, but the variation I prefer is this one with good dark chocolate chunks. These make an excellent nibble alongside a cup of tea (as per the name) or coffee. It is one of the simplest recipes in this chapter and a great way to practice making a tangzhong (see opposite) and rolling perfectly round buns before putting those skills to work in the more complex recipes later in the chapter with cream-filled centers or more challenging shapes. MAKES 18 BUNS

Butter for greasing

Soft Bun Dough (opposite)

6 ounces (170 g) 63% (or higher) bittersweet chocolate, chopped (see Note, page 60)

2 teaspoons freshly ground decorticated cardamom (see page 21)

Flour for dusting

To finish

1 egg

Butter a medium bowl.

MAKE THE DOUGH

Follow the directions on the opposite page until the sugar and butter are incorporated. Add the chocolate and cardamom and continue to knead with the dough hook for 2 minutes more.

Transfer the dough to the prepared bowl. Cover it with a clean kitchen towel or plastic wrap and chill it overnight (up to 12 hours) in the refrigerator or let it rest and rise at room temperature for 1 to 2 hours. After the dough has rested, it will look puffier and feel slightly drier to the touch.

Line two 13 by 18-inch (33 by 46 cm) baking trays with parchment paper.

Lightly dust a work surface with flour. Divide the dough into eighteen balls of approximately 80 g each. I recommend forming three equal-size logs. Then portion each log into six pieces using your bench scraper (see page 37). (For precision, use a digital scale.) Clean any residual dough off of your work surface with the bench scraper, then lightly dust again with flour.

To form the buns, hold your hand in a relaxed claw shape, gently curling your fingers over a ball of dough. While placing very light pressure on the ball, rub your wrist and fingertips repeatedly in a circular motion against the work surface, holding the dough loosely as you feel it become rounder and smoother. Once you're satisfied with the shape of the ball, place it on one of the prepared baking trays and repeat this forming technique with the remaining dough balls. You should have nine buns on each baking tray, spaced a few inches (7 to 9 cm) apart.

CONTINUED

PROOF THE BUNS

Cover the buns with a kitchen towel and set them in a warm and draft-free area until they are noticeably puffier, slightly dry looking, and the impression of a fingerprint is slow to fill in, 1 to 2 hours, depending on the temperature of your kitchen. For an alternate method that takes less time but requires a more watchful eye, see "Proofing Dough" on page 36.

When the buns are sufficiently proofed, preheat the oven to 350°F (175°C).

In a small bowl, whisk the egg with a fork. Using a pastry brush, lightly brush each bun with the egg wash, coating the entire surface.

Bake for 25 to 30 minutes, rotating the baking trays halfway through from top to bottom and front to back, until they are golden brown.

Let the buns cool slightly before serving. The buns are best enjoyed on the day they are baked. Or you can store them in an airtight container, where they will stay fresh for up to 3 days; just cut them in half like a bagel, then give them a good toast and a slather of butter. They can also be frozen and thawed, then reheated in the oven or toaster to freshen them up.

CINNAMON KNOTS

Kanelbullar

The fall is a festive but hectic season in my family when all three of my children and two of my closest friends have birthdays. By the end of it, I've usually had more than my fair share of streamers, popping balloons, and layer cakes. While Danes prefer delicious, airy whipped cream and fresh fruit layer cakes to be served at birthday parties, according to my Swedish friends there's no need to eat cake at all. Instead, a special day like this calls for Swedish cinnamon knots. When you taste these, you may agree. Unlike the American cinnamon buns that I grew up on in Ohio, traditional Swedish cinnamon knots have no icing and just a sprinkle of crunchy sugar on top. These knots are chewy and succulent, with a unique shaping technique that resembles a pile of silky ribbons. MAKES 12 KNOTS

Soft Bun Dough (page 110)

Flour for dusting

Filling

½ cup plus 3 tablespoons (155 g) unsalted butter, at room temperature

¾ cup (160 g) packed light brown sugar

1 heaping tablespoon ground cinnamon

½ teaspoon kosher salt

To finish

1 egg

3 tablespoons Swedish pearl sugar (see page 25)

MAKE THE DOUGH

Follow the directions on page 110 until the sugar and butter are incorporated. Cover the dough with a clean kitchen towel or plastic wrap and chill it overnight (up to 12 hours) in the refrigerator or let it rest and rise at room temperature for 1 to 2 hours, until you are ready to shape it.

MAKE THE FILLING

In the bowl of a stand mixer fitted with the paddle attachment, beat the butter, brown sugar, cinnamon, and salt on medium for 2 to 3 minutes, until it forms a brown paste. (The goal is simply to combine the ingredients, not to cream them or incorporate air.)

When you are ready to make the cinnamon knots, line two 13 by 18-inch (33 by 46 cm) baking trays with parchment paper and lightly dust a work surface with flour.

Transfer the dough to the prepared work surface and roll it into a 12 by 20-inch (30 by 50 cm) rectangle, situated so that the short (12-inch/30 cm) end is closest to you, parallel to the edge of your work surface. Gently pinch and tug the corners to square off the edges to the best of your ability.

Visualize the rectangle in horizontal thirds. Using an offset or rubber spatula, spread the filling over the lower two-thirds of the dough, leaving the top one-third bare (see photographs, page 114). Fold the top third down onto the middle third, then fold the bottom third up over that. (This ensures that there is a layer of dough followed by a layer of topping followed by a layer of dough.)

CONTINUED

Ensure that you have a 12-inch-long (30 cm) pastry strip. If not, gently roll it out or push in the edges until you get the proper length. Score twelve marks at 1-inch (2.5 cm) intervals with the edge of a knife or bench scraper, then, using the scores as a guide, cut the pastry into strips with a pizza wheel or chef's knife (see photograph, below).

MAKE THE KNOTS

Lightly dust your work surface again with flour, making sure you have a few feet to work in each direction. Hold the end of one strip of dough between your thumb, index finger, and middle finger. Lay the rest of the strip on your work surface and roll the palm of your other hand over the strip to twist it six or seven times, spiraling toward the hand that is pinching the other end. With the hand that's holding the dough, wrap the twisted dough around your three fingers twice. Poke the end of the strip into the center of the knot to secure and hide it (see photographs, page 116). Repeat with the remaining strips.

Place the knots about 3 inches (7.5 cm) apart on the prepared baking trays, six per tray.

CONTINUED

NOTE You can freeze the knots immediately after shaping them for up to 1 week, either wrapped on a tray or in an airtight container, with parchment between layers. Remove them from the freezer to thaw and proof right before baking. This makes them a great choice if you know that you want to include them as part of a special meal, especially a breakfast or brunch on a morning when you might not have time to undertake a multiple-stage baking project.

PROOF THE KNOTS

Cover the knots with a kitchen towel and set them in a warm and draft-free area until they are noticeably puffier, slightly dry looking, and the impression of a fingerprint is slow to fill in, 1 to 2 hours, depending on the temperature of your kitchen. For an alternate method that takes less time but requires a more watchful eye, see "Proofing Dough" on page 36.

When the knots are sufficiently proofed, preheat the oven to 350°F (175°C).

In a small bowl, whisk the egg with a fork. Using a pastry brush, lightly brush each knot with the egg wash, coating the entire surface. Sprinkle each knot with the pearl sugar.

Bake for 20 to 25 minutes, rotating the baking trays halfway through from top to bottom and front to back, until they are golden brown all over. Let the knots cool slightly before serving. These cinnamon knots are best enjoyed on the day they are baked. Or you can store them in an airtight container, where they will stay fresh for 2 to 3 days; just preheat the oven to 350°F (175°C) and pop them in for 10 to 12 minutes to freshen them up.

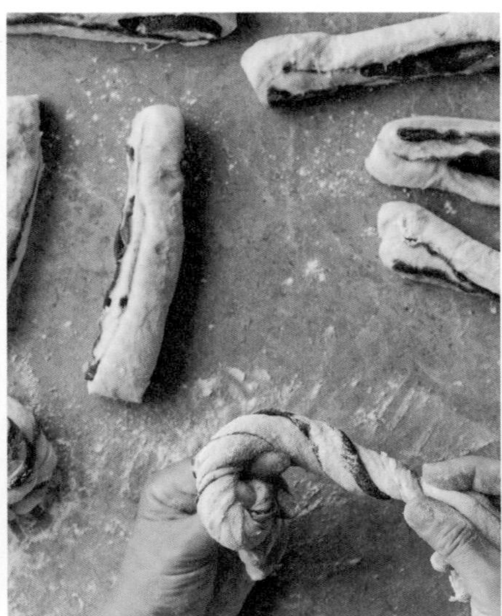

CHOCOLATE-COVERED CUSTARD BUNS

Fastelavnsboller

Not long after settling in Denmark, I was hired to work as a chef in a school kitchen and tasked with making food for 240 kids daily. One day, the head of the school approached me and told me about Fastelavn, a holiday I'd never heard of. Pronounced "fast-eh-laun," Fastelavn means "the evening before Lent." In the old days, Scandinavian people used to abstain from sweets for the entire forty days of Lent, and so they got their fill beforehand by filling their bellies with all of the treats they were going to miss eating. Nowadays, most Danes no longer fast for Lent, so Fastelavn has become a children's festival. On that day, kids dress up in costumes, swing bats at hanging candy-filled barrels, and eat luscious custard-filled and chocolate-glazed buns.

The head of the school asked if I could make these buns for all 240 kids, and I said yes, intrigued by the challenge but also daunted as I had no idea how to fill a bun with custard (let alone 240 buns!). I read recipe after recipe, struggling because my Danish was not yet very good, and called my Danish mother-in-law, who offered to help me make the giant batch of buns. I'm proud to report that all of those kids got their sweet buns, and I learned how to fill buns with custard. **MAKES 12 BUNS**

Soft Bun Dough (page 110)

Pastry cream (see page 92)

Flour for dusting

Chocolate glaze

½ cup (113 g) heavy cream

4 ounces (113 g) 63% (or higher) bittersweet chocolate, broken or chopped into small pieces (see Note, page 60)

MAKE THE DOUGH

Follow the directions on page 110 until the sugar and butter have been incorporated. Cover the dough with a clean kitchen towel or plastic wrap and chill it overnight (up to 12 hours) in the refrigerator or let it rest and rise at room temperature for 1 to 2 hours, until you are ready to shape it.

Line two 13 by 18-inch (33 by 46 cm) baking trays with parchment paper.

Make the pastry cream following the directions on page 92. Transfer the pastry cream to a bowl and place a piece of plastic wrap directly onto the surface of the cream. Chill the cream for at least 30 minutes in the refrigerator.

Lightly dust a work surface with flour. Roll the dough into a 13 by 17-inch (33 by 43 cm) rectangle, gently pinching and pulling at the corners to square them off as much as possible. Using a ruler and a chef's knife or pizza cutter, cut the dough into a 3 by 4-inch (7.5 by 10 cm) grid (for twelve rectangles total).

In the center of each rectangle, place 1 heaping tablespoon of the pastry cream. Gather the corners of the dough together, pinching them

so that you seal the custard inside the dough, almost as if you were making a dumpling. You can pick it up and cradle it in the palm of your hand as you seal it. Place the bun seam side down on one of the prepared baking trays. Repeat with the remaining rectangles of dough. You should have six buns per tray, spaced 2 to 3 inches (5 to 7.5 cm) apart.

PROOF THE BUNS

Cover the buns with a kitchen towel and set them in a warm and draft-free area until they are noticeably puffier, slightly dry looking, and the impression of a fingerprint is slow to fill in, 1 to 2 hours, depending on the temperature of your kitchen. For an alternate method that takes less time but requires a more watchful eye, see "Proofing Dough" on page 36.

When the buns are sufficiently proofed, preheat the oven to 350°F (175°C).

Bake for about 20 minutes, rotating the baking trays halfway through from top to bottom and front to back, until pale brown. Transfer the buns to a rack to cool.

WHILE THE BUNS ARE COOLING, MAKE THE GLAZE

In a small saucepan over medium heat, bring the cream to a gentle simmer, turning the heat off as soon as you see bubbles forming at the edge of the pan. Whisk the chocolate into the cream, continuing to stir as it melts and forms a silky glaze. (If needed, you can turn the stove back on for 1 to 2 minutes, but turn it off again as soon as the chocolate is almost entirely melted.)

Dip the top of each cooled bun into the glaze and allow them to set before serving. These buns are best enjoyed on the day they are baked.

ROASTED RHUBARB AND CREAM CHEESE TARTS

Rhubarb is a favorite summer fruit of mine. The raw stalks appear deceptively celery-like, but stewed, baked, or roasted, it gets transformed into something soft and fragrant and juicy, with a luscious shade of deep pink. In Denmark, I was thrilled to inherit a couple of rhubarb plants that had been planted in our yard by the previous owners. I got really upset when my husband went on a pruning spree one year and I couldn't see any sign of them in the garden after he was done. But then the next spring they came back, and I was inspired to create new recipes.

The shell for these tarts is made from the same dough that goes into the Cinnamon Knots (page 113) and Dark Chocolate Tea Buns (page 111). You form buns and then roll them flat, topping each with lemony cream cheese filling and strips of baked rhubarb. The result is breadier than tarts made with a flaky pie dough. These make a gorgeous seasonal treat for afternoon tea or a summertime dessert (where I'd definitely add a dollop of whipped cream). Both the baked rhubarb and the cream cheese filling can be made ahead of time, allowing you to assemble these rapidly on the day you wish to serve them. Note that while you can cook and eat both red and green parts of rhubarb stalks, the redder they are, the sweeter they will taste. If your rhubarb is pale or greenish, add more sugar. **MAKES TEN 6-INCH (15 CM) INDIVIDUAL TARTS**

Soft Bun Dough (page 110)

Baked rhubarb

10 ounces (280 g) rhubarb stalks, leaves removed, cut into 4-inch (10 cm) pieces

Juice of ½ lemon

3 tablespoons granulated sugar

Cream cheese filling

8 ounces (226 g) cream cheese, at room temperature

⅓ cup (75 g) granulated sugar

1 egg yolk

1 teaspoon fresh lemon juice

½ teaspoon vanilla extract

To finish

Flour for dusting

1 egg

1 tablespoon demerara sugar

MAKE THE DOUGH

Follow the directions on page 110 until the sugar and butter are incorporated. Cover the dough with a clean kitchen towel or plastic wrap and chill it overnight (up to 12 hours) in the refrigerator or let it rest and rise at room temperature for 1 to 2 hours, until you are ready to shape it.

PREPARE THE RHUBARB

Preheat the oven to 350°F (175°C). Place the rhubarb in a small casserole or oven-safe glass dish. Squeeze the lemon juice over the top and then sprinkle the granulated sugar evenly across the surface of each stalk. Bake for 10 to 20 minutes, until slightly softened and juicy. (The baking time will vary depending on the thickness of your stalks and their hydration.) Don't cook them completely because they will bake more once they're added to the tarts. Remove the rhubarb from the oven, leaving the oven on, and set aside to cool.

WHILE THE RHUBARB COOLS, MAKE THE FILLING

In the bowl of a stand mixer fitted with the paddle attachment or in a large bowl with a handheld mixer, beat the cream cheese, sugar, egg yolk, lemon juice, and vanilla until well blended and creamy.

CONTINUED

Once the rhubarb is cool enough to handle, slice each stalk lengthwise into four or five pieces.

Line two 13 by 18-inch (33 by 46 cm) baking trays with parchment paper.

Lightly dust a work surface with flour and divide the dough into ten equal portions. (To be extra precise, use your digital scale.) Roll each portion into a ball, then use your palms to pat and flatten each ball of dough. Using a rolling pin, roll each ball into a 6-inch (15 cm) circle. Transfer the disks of dough to the prepared baking trays. You should have five disks per baking tray, spaced at least 1 inch (2.5 cm) apart.

In a small bowl, whisk the egg with a fork. Using a pastry brush, lightly brush the entire surface of each disk with the egg wash, focusing especially on the edges. Spread each disk evenly with the cream cheese mixture, leaving a ½-inch (1 cm) border. Then arrange the rhubarb matchsticks across the surface of the cream cheese, keeping the strips parallel. Sprinkle the tops with the demerara sugar.

Bake for 20 to 25 minutes, rotating the baking trays halfway through from top to bottom and front to back. Transfer the tarts to a wire rack to cool. These tarts are best enjoyed on the day they are baked.

CARDAMOM WREATH

Kardemommekrans

This cardamom wreath, inspired by Kantine's popular cardamom buns, will be the highlight of your next brunch or fika gathering, a stunning centerpiece for any dining table. A rich paste of pungent freshly ground cardamom, butter, and brown sugar gets slathered over the surface of the brioche dough, which is rolled up, twisted, and formed into a wreath shape. Making the wreath is surprisingly easy and quite forgiving. As the dough rises, it will puff up and erase imperfections, and whatever filling oozes onto the pan will bake into a delicious cardamom brittle that you can nibble on while waiting for your pastry to cool.

The following recipe is the same as the master recipe for Soft Bun Dough (page 110) but halved, as a full recipe would yield a wreath too large to bake on any standard-size baking tray. If you prefer to make a full recipe so that you can create two wreaths and freeze one (or both) for later, then follow the directions for the full batch of bun dough and don't forget to double the filling. If you are planning a larger event or meal, you could also make a full batch of the dough, then use half to create the wreath and the other half to make a half recipe of one of the other recipes in this chapter. MAKES 1 WREATH (ENOUGH FOR 8 TO 10 SERVINGS)

Tangzhong

1 tablespoon plus 1 teaspoon all-purpose flour

¼ cup (60 g) whole milk

Dough

¼ cup (56 g) unsalted butter, cut into 1-inch (2.5 cm) pieces at room temperature, plus more for greasing

1 egg

¾ cup (180 g) whole milk

2¼ cups (288 g) all-purpose flour, plus more for dusting

1 teaspoon kosher salt

1½ teaspoons active dry yeast

3 tablespoons granulated sugar

→ INGREDIENTS CONTINUED

MAKE THE TANGZHONG

In a small saucepan, whisk the flour and milk so that there are no lumps. Cook over medium heat, whisking constantly, until the mixture becomes elastic, with the consistency of thick glue, about 1 minute. Transfer the mixture to the bowl of a stand mixer and let it cool completely, about 10 minutes.

MAKE THE DOUGH

Butter a medium bowl.

In a small bowl, whisk the egg with a fork.

To the mixer bowl with the tangzhong, add the milk, flour, salt, half of the whisked egg (about 2 tablespoons, reserving the remaining half for an egg wash), and the yeast. Using the dough hook attachment, mix on low until all the ingredients are combined, pausing to scrape the sides and bottom of the bowl with a rubber spatula. Increase the speed to medium and mix for 4 minutes more. Decrease the speed to low and sprinkle in the granulated sugar, 1 tablespoon at a time. Gradually add the butter, one or two pieces at a time, waiting between each addition for them to be incorporated into the dough, then mix for 4 minutes more. The butter should be completely absorbed into a glossy and stretchy dough that is beginning to come off the sides of the bowl. Don't worry if it looks quite wet; it will firm up as it sits and rises.

CONTINUED

Transfer the dough to the prepared bowl. Cover it with a kitchen towel or plastic wrap and chill it overnight (up to 12 hours) in the refrigerator or let it rest and rise at room temperature for 1 to 2 hours, until you are ready to shape it.

Cardamom filling

⅓ cup (75 g) unsalted butter, at room temperature

¼ cup (50 g) packed light brown sugar

¼ cup (50 g) granulated sugar

1 tablespoon freshly ground decorticated cardamom (see page 21)

Pinch of kosher salt

To finish

3 tablespoons Swedish pearl sugar (see page 25)

WHILE YOUR DOUGH IS RESTING, MAKE THE FILLING

In the bowl of a stand mixer fitted with the paddle attachment or in a medium bowl using a spatula, beat the butter, brown sugar, granulated sugar, cardamom, and salt on medium speed for 2 to 3 minutes, until it forms a brown paste. (The goal is simply to combine the ingredients, not to cream them or incorporate air.)

Line a 13 by 18-inch (33 by 46 cm) baking tray with parchment paper.

Lightly dust a work surface with flour and roll the dough into a 10 by 15-inch (25 by 38 cm) rectangle, with one short end near the edge of the work surface, closest to you. It doesn't have to be perfectly shaped, but it should come close to those dimensions. Try your best to roll it to a uniform thickness and gently pinch and pull at the corners to square them off.

Using a rubber or offset spatula, evenly smear the entire surface with the cardamom filling and then roll the dough up lengthwise like a jelly roll. Roll the entire piece to even and lengthen it out to about 20 inches (50 cm) long.

With a chef's knife, cut the roll in half lengthwise. I usually start cutting from the middle down, then return and cut the rest of the way from the middle up. Turn the cut sides to face upward, exposing the stripes of cardamom filling.

Pinch the two long strands together at one end, and begin gently laying the strands one on top of the other, twisting them while trying to keep the cut sides (with the visible ribbons of filling) facing upward as much as possible (see photographs on page 126). Keep twisting until you reach the end. Then pinch the ends together to form a ring.

Bring the prepared baking tray as close to your work surface as possible and carefully transfer the wreath onto it. Your wreath may need a little reshaping once you've placed it on the tray, but don't fuss too much as most irregularities will vanish as the wreath proofs and bakes. The wreath should measure about 9 inches (23 cm) across.

CONTINUED

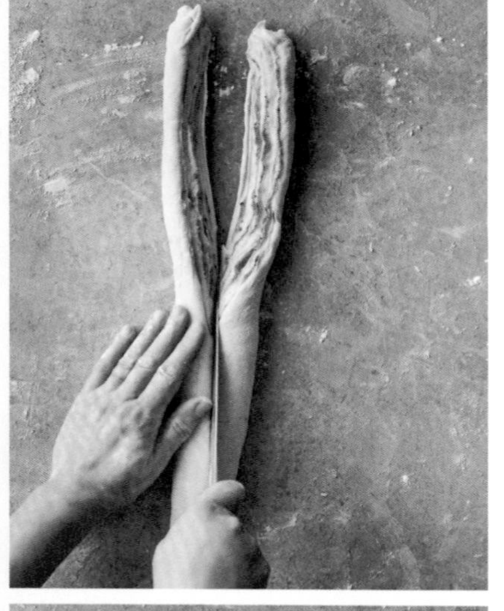

CARDAMOM WREATH, CONTINUED

PROOF THE WREATH

Cover the wreath with a kitchen towel and set them in a warm and draft-free area until they are noticeably puffier, slightly dry looking, and the impression of a fingerprint is slow to fill in, 1 to 2 hours, depending on the temperature of your kitchen. For an alternate method that takes less time but requires a more watchful eye, see "Proofing Dough" on page 36.

When the wreath is sufficiently proofed, preheat the oven to 350°F (175°C).

Whisk the remaining beaten egg with 1 tablespoon water. Using a pastry brush, lightly brush the top of the wreath with the egg wash, then evenly sprinkle the pearl sugar over it.

Bake for 35 to 40 minutes, rotating the baking tray halfway through, until the wreath is puffed and a deep golden brown. Let the wreath cool slightly on the baking tray before transferring it to a rack. Once the wreath is cool enough to handle, transfer it to a platter and bring it out to the table so that everyone can *ooh* and *ahh* in admiration before you slice it into eight to ten pieces for serving. The cardamom wreath is best enjoyed on the day it is baked. Or you can store it in an airtight container, where it will stay fresh for 1 day; just pop it in a 350°F (175°C) oven for 5 to 10 minutes to warm it up again.

NOTE Many people are too busy on a holiday morning or right before a special event to go through all of the steps needed to make a cardamom wreath. You can make and shape the wreath the day before you want to serve it, leaving it in the refrigerator overnight, ready to proof the following morning. You can also shape the wreath up to a week in advance and freeze it on a baking tray lined with parchment, wrapped in plastic, until the day before serving. The night before you're ready to bake it, thaw it in the refrigerator. The proofing time for the thawed pastry is 1 to 2½ hours, depending on the temperature of your kitchen.

SEMLOR

Historically, Swedish semlor (semla in singular form) were similar in texture to hot dog buns that were soaked in hot sweetened milk. Thank goodness the recipe has evolved over the years! This is the recipe that Helena and I developed together (see page 130). It's similar to my Soft Bun Dough (page 110) but with a few necessary tweaks. Once baked, you snip a "lid" off the top of each bun using scissors and then scoop out some of the sweet and tender breadcrumbs, which get mixed together with almond paste and a touch of milk before being spooned back in. You then cover the filling with a mound of unsweetened whipped cream before the lid is placed on the bun. They're an example of over-the-top luxuriousness and look as beautiful as they are delicious. **MAKES 12 BUNS**

Tangzhong

3 tablespoons all-purpose flour

½ cup (120 g) whole milk

Dough

¾ cup (180 g) whole milk, at room temperature

3 cups (384 g) all-purpose flour, plus more for dusting

2½ teaspoons active dry yeast

1 teaspoon freshly ground decorticated cardamom (see page 21)

Pinch of kosher salt

1 egg

⅓ cup (80 g) granulated sugar

⅓ cup (76 g) unsalted butter, at room temperature

→ INGREDIENTS CONTINUED

MAKE THE TANGZHONG

In a small saucepan, whisk the flour and milk so that there are no lumps. Cook over medium heat, whisking constantly, until the mixture becomes elastic, with the consistency of thick glue, about 1 minute. Transfer the mixture to the bowl of a stand mixer and let it cool completely, about 10 minutes.

MAKE THE DOUGH

To the mixer bowl with the tangzhong, add the milk, flour, yeast, cardamom, salt, and egg. Using the dough hook attachment, mix on low, gradually increasing the speed to medium as the ingredients are incorporated, 6 minutes. During the last minute, add the granulated sugar and mix until combined, followed by the butter, about 1 tablespoon at a time. Mix for 2 minutes more, pause to scrape the sides and bottom of the bowl with a rubber spatula, and mix for 1 minute more. This will be a very wet dough. Let it rest for 5 minutes.

Transfer the dough to a medium bowl. Cover it with plastic wrap and chill for at least 30 minutes, until cold, or overnight (up to 12 hours) in the refrigerator.

Line two 13 by 18-inch (33 by 46 cm) baking trays with parchment paper.

Lightly dust a work surface with flour. Divide the dough into twelve balls of approximately 75 g each (for precision, use a digital scale; see page 37).

To form the buns, hold your hand in a relaxed claw shape, gently curling your fingers over a ball of dough. While placing very light pressure on

Filling

¾ cup (220 g) almond paste (see page 21)

½ cup (100 g) granulated sugar

1 teaspoon kosher salt

½ cup (118 g) whole milk

To finish

2 cups (480 g) heavy cream

Powdered sugar for sprinkling

the ball, rub your wrist and fingertips repeatedly in a circular motion against the work surface, holding the dough loosely within your palm as you feel it become rounder and smoother. Once you're satisfied with the shape of the ball, place it on one of the prepared baking trays and repeat this forming technique with the remaining dough balls. I suggest using a bench scraper to clean the counter after each ball, as it's much easier to roll them without traces of dough stuck to the counter. You should have six buns per baking tray, spaced a few inches (about 7 cm) apart.

PROOF THE BUNS

Cover the buns with a kitchen towel and set them in a warm and draft-free area until they are noticeably puffier, slightly dry looking, and the impression of a fingerprint is slow to fill in, 1 to 2 hours, depending on the temperature of your kitchen. For an alternate method that takes less time but requires a more watchful eye, see "Proofing Dough" on page 36.

When the buns are sufficiently proofed, preheat the oven to 400°F (200°C).

Bake for 12 to 15 minutes, rotating the baking trays halfway through from top to bottom and front to back, until they are golden brown. Let them cool completely on a rack.

ONCE THEY HAVE COOLED, MAKE THE FILLING

Use kitchen scissors or a small paring knife to cut a rather large (about 1½ inches/3.5 cm on each side) triangle into the top of each bun, setting aside the "lid." Use a fork to scrape out about 2 tablespoons of stuffing from each bun, transferring it to the bowl of a stand mixer fitted with the whisk attachment. Pinch off any of the crumbs adhered to the bottom of the lid and add them to the bowl as well. You should end up with about 3 cups (160 g) of brioche crumbs. Be precise here. If you don't have enough, the mixture will be too watery, and so more crumbs would need to be scooped from the buns. Add the almond paste, sugar, and salt and mix on low. Add the milk, increasing the speed just slightly. You want the filling to come together so that it's almost fluid and pipeable. Taste and add another pinch of salt, if desired.

In the bowl of a stand mixer fitted with the whisk attachment, whip the cream on medium until soft peaks form (see page 37). Transfer the whipped cream to a piping bag fitted with a star-shaped tip.

Carefully spoon the almond filling into the buns, dividing it equally and filling each cavity completely. (To fill the buns more neatly, you could also transfer the filling to a second piping bag, if you have one, or a zip-top bag with one corner snipped off.) Then pipe the whipped cream over the filling. Don't skimp on the whipped cream, and make sure that you cover each hole completely. Put the lids back on and sift powdered sugar over each bun.

Semlor are best enjoyed on the day they are baked.

A FRIENDSHIP FORGED OVER BUNS

The semla (semlor in plural) is arguably the most popular pastry in Sweden. Soft and sweet buns get hollowed and filled with an almond paste filling. These are Sweden's version of the Chocolate-Covered Custard Buns (page 117), both of which were traditionally made in the days leading up to Fastelavn, also known as Fat Tuesday, the day before Lent begins, with the tradition of gorging on sweets before having to abstain until Easter. Nowadays, however, semlor are so popular that the season has stretched out, and they start appearing in bakeries shortly after Christmas. In fact, I know of a few Stockholm bakeries that now make them year-round!

When I opened Kantine, I wanted to serve semlor in January and February. I had not yet perfected my recipe when I got an interesting call. The head of San Francisco's Scandinavian preschool knew of a passionate Swedish baker named Helena Bjernekull who was visiting San Francisco and looking for a place to stage, which means spending a short period of time as a guest chef or baker in a restaurant kitchen, cooking and learning the way they work to gain inspiration and knowledge. I invited Helena to have a bite to eat at Kantine, and we hit it off right away. As it turns out, Helena was working at Sweden's Michelin-starred (and now defunct) restaurant Fäviken under head chef Magnus Nilsson. The semla recipe became our shared project.

It was Helena's fabulous suggestion to use freshly ground decorticated cardamom instead of the preground stuff sold at supermarkets, a technique I have since imported into my other baked goods. Prior to that, I hadn't realized what a dramatic difference using freshly ground cardamom would make. She also adjusted my existing dough recipe to include less flour. As a result, it's slightly stickier and a bit harder to handle, but the result is so tender and scrumptious it's worth the effort. We agreed that the whipped cream should be unsweetened because the almond paste mixture is so sugary that they balance each other out.

Helena baked with us for the majority of her vacation in San Francisco. A couple of years later, I went to visit her at Fäviken the summer before it closed for good, and the experience was like a dream come true. We got to bake bread there, I stayed at her house, and she's remained a dear friend. I love these connections and community that come out of baking, and I always think of her as I bake tray after tray of these luxurious semlor, which have proven just as popular in San Francisco as in Sweden.

In keeping with tradition, Fat Tuesday is the last day, after about a six-week run, that we offer semlor in the pastry case at Kantine. And last year, when we announced that our semla season was coming to an end, orders came flooding in so fast that I feared we would sell out before opening. Thankfully, our team baked them tirelessly beginning in the early dawn and we managed to keep filling the demand into the afternoon. What a sweet way to end the semla season!

At Kantine, we have created several semla variations using the same bun dough, and although they can't technically be called semlor, they are just as luscious as the original. I've included my favorite, Lemon Curd and Cream Buns (page 133), for lemon lovers, like me.

LEMON CURD AND CREAM BUNS

This recipe was inspired by a lemon bun that I had at Juno, which is hands down my favorite bakery in Copenhagen. When Juno first opened, they had a super cramped little space: just a door, a counter, and a tiny baking area. Every morning a line stretched around the corner, and they changed the menu so often that you never knew exactly what they'd have. Juno blew my mind because they seemed to master both naturally leavened breads and gorgeous pastries under one roof. I remember one time purchasing a sourdough bun that was still warm as I ate it while walking away, the fresh butter melting into the bread. Tears literally sprang into my eyes as I contemplated how something so simple could be so good. (But I digress!)

I fell in love with their lemon buns on a recent trip to Copenhagen, when my friend Paula Holm and I were on one of our pastry crawls. Attempting to re-create these buns at home, I realized the semla bun recipe worked beautifully when paired with a zingy lemon curd I'd created with inspiration from Serena Bass's lemon curd cake recipe (lemon lovers, you've got to bake that one too!). The tender bun, the tart curd, the velvety cream, it's a luxurious treat that I'm simply unable to resist! **MAKES 12 BUNS**

12 Semlor (page 127)

2 tablespoons sugar

Lemon curd filling

⅓ cup (65 g) sugar

¼ teaspoon kosher salt

Zest of 2 lemons, finely grated

⅓ cup (76 g) juice (from 3 to 4 lemons; Eureka lemons are typical, but Meyer lemons would make a fun variation)

3 egg yolks

1 egg

3 tablespoons unsalted butter, at room temperature, diced

Simple syrup

¼ cup (85 g) water

¼ cup (50 g) sugar

To finish

Finely grated zest of 2 lemons

MAKE THE BUNS

Follow the directions for making the dough and baking the buns on page 127. Let the buns cool completely on a rack.

MAKE THE LEMON CURD

In a nonreactive medium pot, combine the sugar, salt, about one-third of the lemon zest, and the lemon juice and whisk until smooth. Add the egg yolks and the egg and whisk to combine. Place the pot on the stove over medium-low heat and stir until the mixture begins to bubble around the edges. Add the butter, one piece at a time, stirring after each addition. Decrease the heat to low and stir constantly as the butter melts and the mixture simmers for about 5 minutes, until it coats the back of a wooden spoon. Transfer the curd to a large bowl and place a piece of plastic wrap directly onto the surface of the curd to keep it from forming a skin. Chill the curd in the refrigerator until cold. (Lemon curd keeps for up to 2 weeks in an airtight container in the refrigerator, so this can be made in advance if desired.)

CONTINUED

MAKE THE SIMPLE SYRUP

In a small saucepan over medium-high heat, heat the water and sugar until the sugar melts, about 5 minutes. Remove from the heat and let the syrup cool completely.

It's time to fill the buns. A favorite trick of mine is to use the wide end of a piping tip as a small round cutter to make a perfectly round hole in the bottom of each bun, reserving the bread "corks" from your piping tip to close the holes up once the buns have been filled. If you don't have a piping tip, use a pair of kitchen scissors or a small paring knife to carefully open the bottom of a bun. Once you've gained access to the inside of the bun, use your fingers or a fork to create space for the filling, removing about 2 teaspoons of crumbs from inside each bun.

MAKE THE FILLING

In the bowl of a stand mixer fitted with the whisk attachment or in a large bowl with a handheld mixer, whip the cream on medium until soft peaks form, being careful not to overwhip it (see page 37). Fold the cream into the chilled lemon curd. Transfer the lemon curd filling to a pastry bag fitted with a star-shaped tip. Insert the pastry tip into each bun opening and squeeze in as much pastry cream as you can. Each should hold about 1 tablespoon. Close up your buns with the "corks," flip them over, and set them on a rack.

Place the sugar in a medium bowl. Lightly brush the filled buns with simple syrup. Toss each bun in the sugar so it adheres to the damp surface of the bun. Let them dry on a rack or baking tray for about 10 minutes.

To finish the buns, pipe a dime-size star of cream on the top of each bun and garnish with a tiny sprinkle of the lemon zest. These lemon cream buns are best enjoyed on the day they are baked.

MASTER RECIPE: DANISH DOUGH/ WIENERBRØD

Danish dough is "laminated," meaning that a sheet of butter gets folded between layers of leavened dough, rolled out, and then folded and rolled again several times with breaks to chill in the refrigerator. This process creates thinner and thinner layers of pastry dough surrounding thinner and thinner layers of butter, which leads to all of those flaky and delectable baked layers that make danishes so divine. Croissants and puff pastry are also made of laminated dough, but the ingredients differ; they don't contain eggs, for instance, while danishes do.

Making laminated dough is not difficult, but it does take time (much of which is chilling time), precision (a good ruler is essential), and care. When the butter is enclosed in the dough, you want to roll it out gently, especially as the dough thins, so that it doesn't tear and seep through. You also want to do your best to roll and shape the dough into a rectangle with 90-degree corners and fold it tightly around the butter, which has to be at the right temperature.

That said, I've taught inexperienced bakers how to make this dough, and it's surprisingly forgiving. If making homemade danishes sounds like fun to you, then dive in. Also, even an imperfect danish still tastes great. I'm sharing recipes that feature a few classic shapes that danish dough often takes—a morning bun, snails, twists, and a braid—but once you get comfortable making this laminated danish dough, there's no limit to what you could create out of it, both sweet and savory.

One added bonus to the extra effort it takes to make this flaky dough is that pastries made from laminated dough tend to reheat well compared to those made from the simpler brioche dough. If you have some left over, store them in an airtight container until ready to enjoy, then heat them for 5 to 10 minutes in a preheated 350°F (175°C) oven.

MAKES 1 "BOOK" OF DANISH DOUGH

- ¾ cup (185 g) whole milk
- 2 eggs
- 2 tablespoons sugar
- 1¾ teaspoons active dry yeast
- 4½ cups (553 g) bread flour, plus more for dusting
- 1 tablespoon kosher salt
- 1¼ cups (282 g) unsalted butter, chilled

In the bowl of a stand mixer, whisk by hand the milk, eggs, sugar, and yeast. Add the flour and salt to the bowl and mix, using the dough hook attachment, on the lowest speed for about 2 minutes. (If you don't have a stand mixer, you could knead the dough by hand.) The dough will look dry and shaggy, but fear not; it will come together eventually. Increase the speed to medium and continue mixing for 4 minutes, or until a firm dough forms. Turn out the dough onto a work surface and give it a few kneading strokes to bring it together into a smooth ball. Cover the surface of the ball with plastic wrap or a kitchen towel and let it rest on the counter for 1 hour or in the refrigerator for a maximum of 4 hours.

After the dough has rested, remove the butter from the refrigerator and let it come to room temperature while you roll out the dough.

Lightly dust a 13 by 18-inch (33 by 46 cm) baking tray with flour.

CONTINUED

MASTER RECIPE: DANISH DOUGH/ WIENERBRØD, CONTINUED

Lightly dust a work surface with flour, then roll the dough into a 10 by 15-inch (25 by 38 cm) rectangle. Try to get fairly close to those dimensions, gently tugging at the corners. Place the dough on the prepared baking tray and put it in the refrigerator while you work with the butter.

Lay out a piece of parchment paper on your work surface. If you're using sticks of butter, cut the butter into tablespoon-size portions (you should end up with twenty pieces) and position them in a rectangular grid on the parchment paper, laying five pieces in one direction and four pieces in the other direction with each piece touching. If you're using butter from a block, cut roughly uniform thick slices to create a 6 by 7-inch (15 by 18 cm) slab of butter. Cover the butter with a second sheet of parchment paper and roll over it gently with a rolling pin. Remove the top piece of parchment paper and, with a bench scraper or offset spatula, scrape the butter block lightly so that it has a smooth surface and a uniform thickness and measures approximately 6 by 9 inches (15 by 22 cm). Place the butter in the refrigerator for about 10 minutes to firm up again.

After 10 minutes, press a fingertip against the top of the butter. It should take some effort to make a depression and feel like touching clay or Play-Doh. You want the butter close to the same softness as the refrigerated dough: soft but not melty, cold but not icy, and still workable.

The first step is to "lock in" the butter. Lightly dust a work surface with flour, then position the 10 by 15-inch (25 by 38 cm) rectangle of dough so that the long (15-inch/38 cm) end is closest to you, parallel to the edge of your work surface. Place the rectangle of butter in the middle of the dough so that the short (6-inch/15 cm) end is parallel to the edge of your work surface. The long (9-inch/22 cm) ends of the butter rectangle should come close to meeting the short (10-inch/25 cm) ends of the dough rectangle, and there should be about 3 inches (7.5 cm) of bare dough to the left and the right of the butter. Fold these two flaps of dough snugly over the butter to enclose it, pinching the center seam, as well as the top and bottom, so that the butter is completely sealed inside the dough. The finished packet should be about 7 by 9 inches (18 by 23 cm). Next, you will be making three folds.

FOLD NO. 1

Gently roll the dough out lengthwise, stretching the long (9-inch/22 cm) side to 18 inches (46 cm). The goal is to make it longer but not much wider so that in the end it measures about 9½ by 18 inches (24 by 46 cm). As you roll, don't push too hard or you risk tearing the dough or squeezing the butter out. Try to do it in more strokes rather than by exerting pressure. Once it measures about 9½ by 18 inches (24 by 46 cm), fold it in thirds, as you would a letter (this is called the "letter" fold). The top third folds down over the middle, and then the bottom third folds up over the middle and the top. The finished packet should be about 6 by 9½ inches (15 by 24 cm). Do your best to shape the corners with 90-degree angles, gently pinching and tugging as needed. Cover the dough in plastic wrap, put it back on the baking tray and refrigerate it for 30 minutes. You can continue using the same piece of plastic wrap for all subsequent steps.

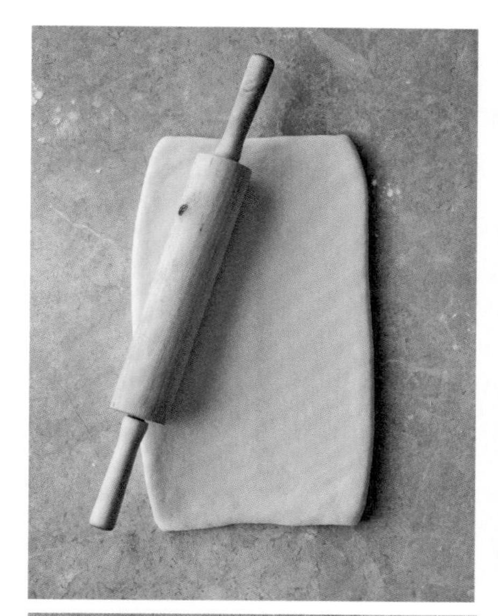

FOLD NO. 2

After 30 minutes, remove the dough from the refrigerator and take off the plastic wrap. Lightly dust the work surface with flour and position the dough with the short (6-inch/15 cm) end closest to you, parallel to the edge of your work surface, and roll it out vertically. Again, work swiftly but be gentle. The goal is to achieve the same measurement as before of approximately 9½ by 18 inches (24 by 46 cm). Then give the dough another letter fold, folding the top third of the dough down over the middle and the bottom third of the dough up over the middle and the top. Pat it together, pinch and square off the corners, cover it with the plastic wrap, put it back on the baking tray and refrigerate it for 45 minutes.

FOLD NO. 3

After 45 minutes, remove the dough from the refrigerator and take off the plastic wrap. Once again, lightly dust the work surface with flour and position the dough with the short (6-inch/15 cm) end closest to you, parallel to the edge of your work surface, and roll it out following the same steps as above, once again aiming for a rectangle that is approximately 9½ by 18 inches (24 by 46 cm). Give the dough a final letter fold. The resulting packet should be about 6 by 9½ inches (15 by 24 cm).

A laminated slab of dough is often referred to as a "book." Books can come in all different sizes (depending on how many pastries need to be made). At this stage, your small book is so close to being ready to use! Last step: Wrap it back up in plastic wrap and let it rest in the refrigerator for at least 1 hour before beginning to shape it. Your book will stay fresh for 12 hours in the refrigerator or up to 1 month in the freezer. If you freeze your book, allow it to thaw in the refrigerator overnight before using.

PEAR AND CHAMOMILE CREAM DANISHES

Foraging is big in Scandinavia, and I've long been a fan of using what's wild in cooking. As long as you're good at identification, it's a fun way to incorporate brilliant flavors into your food. These days, apps on your phone can assist in identification! Whenever I'm in a new place, I go for walks to get inspired. And I often find things in nature that make their way into a dish.

Scandinavia is one place chamomile grows wild. My former neighbors in Copenhagen often witnessed me pulling the rangy plants from cracks in the sidewalk. One of my favorite uses for these flowers is to steep them in milk to make a delicately floral pastry cream, which is featured in these danishes beneath thick slices of roasted pear. If there is no wild chamomile growing near you the dried flowers used for tea will do. Buy them loose in bulk or just snip open a tea bag. In the summer, these chamomile cream danishes are equally delicious with sliced stone fruit like nectarines, peaches, or plums. **MAKES 12 DANISHES**

Danish Dough (page 135)

Flour for dusting

Chamomile pastry cream

2 cups (480 g) whole milk

2 tablespoons dried chamomile flowers

4 egg yolks

⅓ cup (67 g) granulated sugar

1 tablespoon cornstarch

For topping

3 to 4 firm pears

1 tablespoon dried chamomile flowers

2 to 3 tablespoons demerara sugar

MAKE THE DOUGH

Follow the directions on page 135, up to and including fold no. 3. The dough should be chilled and ready to use.

MAKE THE CHAMOMILE PASTRY CREAM

In a small saucepan, combine the milk and chamomile flowers. Place the pan on the stove over medium heat and let the mixture come to a simmer, turning off the heat as soon as you see bubbles forming. Let the milk sit for 20 minutes while the chamomile steeps.

In a small bowl, whisk together the egg yolks, sugar, and cornstarch until it forms a dark yellow paste. Once the chamomile is done steeping, return the pot to the stove over medium-low heat and bring it to a low simmer. Add the hot milk to the egg mixture and whisk together until well combined. Then pour this mixture back into the pot and place it over medium-low heat, whisking continuously as it thickens to a custard. When you hear a *glug glug* sound of bubbles forming, set a timer for 1 minute, and whisk constantly, then remove the pan from the heat. Strain the custard through a fine-mesh strainer into a medium bowl and place a piece of plastic wrap directly onto the surface of the custard. Refrigerate for at least 30 minutes.

Line two 13 by 18-inch (33 by 46 cm) baking trays with parchment paper.

Lightly dust a work surface with flour. Place the book of dough on a work surface with one of the short (6-inch/15 cm) ends close to you, parallel to

The swirl (middle right) for these pear danishes is just one of many ways to shape individual pastries.

the edge of the work surface. Roll the book of dough out, using vertical motions, into a 9 by 16-inch (23 by 40 cm) rectangle. Gently tug and pinch at the corners to square them off as best you can.

Using a ruler, faintly trace lines with the tip of a chef's knife to measure twelve ¾-inch (2 cm) vertical strips. With a chef's knife or pizza cutter, cut out these strips of dough.

Twist the one end of the dough strip until you have a long, even twist. Then, starting at one end, coil the twist into a fat swirl on the counter, where the pastry coils just touch one another but leave room for the dough to expand while proofing. Tuck the tail end underneath the swirl and place it on a prepared baking tray. Repeat this shaping process with the remaining the strips, placing six swirls (spaced approximately 1½ inches/3.5 cm apart) on each baking tray.

PROOF THE DANISHES

Cover the shaped pastries with a kitchen towel and set them in a warm and draft-free area until they are noticeably puffier, slightly dry looking, and the impression of a fingerprint is slow to fill in, 1 to 2 hours, depending on the temperature of your kitchen. For an alternate method that takes less time but requires a more watchful eye, see "Proofing Dough" on page 36.

WHILE THE DANISHES PROOF, PREP THE PEARS

Cut each pear lengthwise into slices ¼ inch (6 mm) thick, and then use a melon baller to neatly remove the seeds at the center.

When the danishes are sufficiently proofed, preheat the oven to 375°F (190°C).

In a small bowl, whisk the egg with a fork. Using a pastry brush, lightly brush the entire surface of each swirl with the egg wash.

Wrap the bottom of a glass or small mug with plastic wrap. Place it on the center of each coil and lightly press and twist, creating an indentation to hold the pastry cream and fruit.

Spoon a dollop of pastry cream into each depression, followed by a slice of pear. With your fingertips, crush the chamomile flowers to decorate the surface and then sprinkle the demerara sugar.

Bake the for 30 minutes, rotating the baking trays halfway through from top to bottom and front to back, until dark golden brown. The danishes are best enjoyed warm on the day they are baked.

CARDAMOM MORNING BUNS

Soon after I moved to San Francisco, I was told where to get the best morning buns, a Bay Area treat that originated at a bakery in Berkeley in the '70s. I loved how tightly coiled the pastry remained after baking, and how the whole gooey thing got tossed in a bowl of zesty sugar. Naturally this led to a desire to create a morning bun of my own. Morning buns are shaped like cinnamon rolls but baked in muffin tins rather than on a baking tray. Because they are made of danish dough, you get endless layers of flaky, buttery goodness spread with a sweet and abundantly spiced filling that oozes out at the gooey center of the bun. To make my morning buns taste Scandinavian, I roll them in cardamom sugar, which sticks to the flaky exterior. Squeezing the buns into muffin tins keeps them nice and tidy, so this could be a fun first project for putting your danish dough to use before experimenting with more complex shapes.

MAKES 12 BUNS

Danish Dough (page 135)

⅓ cup plus 1 tablespoon (90 g) unsalted butter, at room temperature, plus more for greasing

½ cup (100 g) sugar

Pinch of kosher salt

2 teaspoons freshly ground decorticated cardamom (see page 21)

To finish

Flour for dusting

¼ cup (50 g) cardamom sugar (see page 77)

MAKE THE DOUGH

Follow the directions on page 135, up to and including fold no. 3. The dough should be chilled and ready to use.

MAKE THE FILLING

In the bowl of a stand mixer fitted with the paddle attachment, beat the butter, sugar, salt, and cardamom on medium for 1 to 2 minutes, until everything is well incorporated; it should be smooth and creamy. (The goal is simply to combine the ingredients, not to cream them or incorporate air.) Set the filling aside at room temperature to keep it soft and spreadable.

Generously butter a 12-cup muffin tin. Be thorough and apply the butter onto the surface of the tin as well as inside the cups so that the dough won't stick to the surface when it puffs during proofing or baking.

Lightly dust a work surface with flour. Place the dough on a work surface with one of the short (6-inch/15 cm) ends close to you, parallel to the edge of the work surface. Roll the dough out, using vertical (up and down) motions, into a 13 by 18-inch (33 by 46 cm) rectangle, gently tugging and pinching at the corners to square them off as best you can. One short (13-inch/33 cm) end should be closest to you, parallel to the edge of the work surface. Spread the cardamom filling, using an offset spatula, evenly across the entire surface of the dough from one edge to the other in both directions. Roll the dough up widthwise, like a jelly roll, as tightly as possible. Try to keep the length close to the original 13 inches (33 cm). Using a chef's knife, make twelve shallow cuts at 1-inch (2.5 cm) intervals. (Your rolls need to fit inside your muffin tin, where they will expand while proofing, so they should be about 1 inch/2.5 cm wide.) Then cut the roll into slices using the marks you made as a guide. Place each piece into a buttered cup of your muffin tin, with one of the cut sides down.

PROOF THE BUNS

Cover the muffin tin with a kitchen towel and set them in a warm and draft-free area until they are noticeably puffier, slightly dry looking, and the impression of a fingerprint is slow to fill in, 1 to 2 hours, depending on the temperature of your kitchen. For an alternate method that takes less time but requires a more watchful eye, see "Proofing Dough" on page 36.

When the buns are sufficiently proofed, preheat the oven to 375°F (190°C).

Place the muffin tin on a larger baking tray before baking. This is important as butter will ooze over the sides of the pan while the morning buns bake, and you want to catch it before it drips onto the bottom of the oven, where it will scorch and smoke.

Bake for 25 to 30 minutes, until the pastry looks dark golden brown. Let the buns cool for 2 to 3 minutes, then tip the muffin tin onto its side and use an offset spatula to gently pry each bun loose, being careful not to let them uncoil.

Add the cardamom sugar to a small bowl. Roll the surface of each morning bun, top down, in the sugar. Give it a good toss, so that the cardamom sugar sticks to the entire surface. Morning buns are best eaten warm or on the day they are baked. If you have some left over, store them in an airtight container until ready to enjoy, and then remove and heat them for 5 to 10 minutes in a preheated 350°F (175°C) oven. Pastries made from danish dough reheat well.

CHOCOLATE AND ORANGE SNAILS WITH MARIGOLD

Marigolds remind me of the front yard of my childhood home where my mom had a huge bed of wildflowers. Each spring, she'd toss out handfuls of dry seeds, and it was always exciting to see what would pop up. The marigolds, in all shades, were one of my favorites. If only I'd known that they were edible back then! Marigolds have a taste that can be described as a cross between citrus and tarragon, which pairs beautifully with chocolate and orange zest in these snails. If you don't have access to a marigold plant or a grocer that sells flowers for food-making purposes, don't substitute pesticide-sprayed ones from a florist—just omit them altogether. I guarantee your chocolate and orange snails will still be a hit!

Snails are similar to morning buns in that you spread a filling over dough and roll it up tightly before cutting it into individual pastries. But snails are cut more narrowly and baked on a tray rather than in muffin tins. **MAKES 12 SNAILS**

- Danish Dough (page 135)
- 3½ ounces (100 g) 63% (or higher) dark chocolate, chopped (see Note, page 60)
- ¼ cup (60 g) unsalted butter
- ½ cup (50 g) powdered sugar
- 1 teaspoon cocoa powder
- Flour for dusting
- 2 large oranges
- 2 or 3 flowering stalks of food-grade marigold
- 2 to 3 tablespoons demerara sugar for sprinkling

MAKE THE DOUGH

Follow the directions on page 135, up to and including fold no. 3. The dough should be chilled and ready to use.

MAKE THE FILLING

In a small microwave-safe bowl, add the chocolate and butter and microwave for about 90 seconds, until most of the chocolate has melted. The carry-over heat will continue to melt the last remaining bits. (If you don't have a microwave, melt the butter over the stove and then, off the heat, add the chocolate.) Stir occasionally until smooth, and then add the powdered sugar and cocoa powder. Stir everything until incorporated and then set aside.

Line two 13 by 18-inch (33 by 46 cm) baking trays with parchment paper.

Lightly dust a work surface with flour. Place the book of dough on a work surface with one of the short (6-inch/15 cm) ends close to you, parallel to the edge of the work surface. Roll the book of dough out, using vertical (up and down) motions, into a 13 by 18-inch (33 by 46 cm) rectangle, gently tugging and pinching at the corners to square them off as best you can.

CONTINUED

Spread the chocolate filling, using an offset spatula, evenly across the entire surface of the dough from one edge to the other in both directions.

Zest the oranges directly over the chocolate filling, and use an offset spatula to ensure the zest is evenly distributed. Pluck the marigold petals off their base and sprinkle them all over the pastry, reserving a small handful of petals for garnish later.

Roll the dough up widthwise, making the roll as compact as you can. Using a ruler and a chef's knife, make twelve shallow cuts at 1-inch (2.5 cm) intervals. Then cut the roll into slices using the marks you made as a guide. Place six snails evenly spaced on each of the prepared baking trays, with one of the cut sides down. Make sure to position the end pieces with the prettier cut side facing up. Sprinkle the tops with the demerara sugar and add a few more marigold petals on each.

PROOF THE SNAILS

Cover the snails with a kitchen towel and set them in a warm and draft-free area until they are noticeably puffier, slightly dry looking, and the impression of a fingerprint is slow to fill in, 1 to 2 hours, depending on the temperature of your kitchen. For an alternate method that takes less time but requires a more watchful eye, see "Proofing Dough" on page 36.

When the snails are sufficiently proofed, preheat the oven to 350°F (175°C).

Bake for 25 to 30 minutes, rotating the baking trays halfway through from top to bottom and front to back, until the pastry looks dark golden brown and crispy. These snails are best eaten warm or on the day they are baked. If you have some left over, store them in an airtight container until ready to enjoy, and then remove and heat them for 5 to 10 minutes in a preheated 350°F (175°C) oven.

POPPY SEED AND ALMOND PASTRIES

Tebirkes

This ultrapopular Danish pastry tastes a bit like an almond croissant. It is the quintessential pastry in Denmark, a standard available at every bakery (as well as convenience stores and supermarkets), and a decadent treat that I can't live without. The name is easy to pronounce. Just say: tea-beer-kiss! It's relatively simple to make, as well, with a filling that consists of almond paste, butter, sugar, and almond flour and an upper crust of poppy seeds. This rich filling melts in the baking process, and inevitably a little bit oozes out of the ends of the flaky packet of dough, creating an irresistibly crunchy/chewy layer that hardens on the parchment paper. At the bakery, we gather these broken pieces in a tub to add to our Rye Chocolate Chip Cookies (page 60). I would encourage you to do the same, but I somehow doubt that you'll be able to stop yourself from popping them in your mouth. **MAKES 10 TEBIRKES**

Danish Dough (page 135)

Filling

⅓ cup (73 g) unsalted butter, at room temperature

6½ ounces (180 g) almond paste (see page 21)

¼ cup (50 g) sugar

⅓ cup (30 g) almond flour

To finish

Flour for dusting

1 egg

1 cup (140 g) poppy seeds

MAKE THE DOUGH

Follow the directions on page 135, up to and including fold no. 3. The dough should be chilled and ready to use.

MAKE THE FILLING

In the bowl of a stand mixer fitted with the paddle attachment, mix the butter, almond paste, sugar, and almond flour on low until it forms a thick and smooth paste. Set aside.

Line two 13 by 18-inch (33 by 46 cm) baking trays with parchment paper.

Lightly dust a work surface with flour. Position the dough on a work surface with one of the short (6-inch/15 cm) ends close to you, parallel to the edge of the work surface. Roll the dough out, using vertical (up and down) motions, into a 9 by 25-inch (23 by 63 cm) strip, gently tugging and pinching at the corners to square them off as best you can. Reposition the strip of dough horizontally so that the long end is parallel with the edge of your work space.

Transfer the filling to a sheet of parchment paper and, using your fingers, shape and roll it into a 24-inch (60 cm) sausage. It will feel like a sticky putty and should be easy to form in this fashion.

Place the almond filling in the middle of the strip of danish dough, where it should extend very close to each short end. Fold the bottom third of the dough up and over the almond filling and pat it down. Then fold the top third of the dough down, overlapping the bottom piece by 1 inch (2.5 cm).

Flip the strip over, seam side down. Super gently (using only the weight of the rolling pin), flatten it ever so slightly. Using a dry pastry brush, brush off any excess flour (otherwise the flour will affect how well your poppy seeds adhere to the pastry).

In a small bowl, whisk the egg with a fork. Using the same pastry brush, lightly brush the top of the entire strip with the egg wash.

Using a chef's knife, make ten shallow cuts at 2½-inch (6 cm) intervals. Then cut the strip into slices using the marks as your guide.

Pour the poppy seeds into a shallow bowl or container. Dip each slice, egg wash side down, into the seeds. Push gently to make them adhere and then place the tebirkes onto the prepared baking trays, poppy seed side up. You should have five tebirkes, evenly spaced, per baking tray.

PROOF THE TEBIRKES

Cover the tebirkes with a kitchen towel and set them in a warm and draft-free area until they are noticeably puffier, slightly dry looking, and the impression of a fingerprint is slow to fill in, 1 to 2 hours, depending on the temperature of your kitchen. For an alternate method that takes less time but requires a more watchful eye, see "Proofing Dough" on page 36.

When the tebirkes are sufficiently proofed, preheat the oven to 375°F (190°C).

Bake for 25 to 30 minutes, rotating the baking trays halfway through from top to bottom and front to back, until the pastries are dark golden brown and some of the filling has seeped out and caramelized on the parchment paper. These are best eaten warm or on the day they are baked. If you have some left over, store them in an airtight container until ready to enjoy, and then remove and heat them for 5 to 10 minutes in a preheated 350°F (175°C) oven.

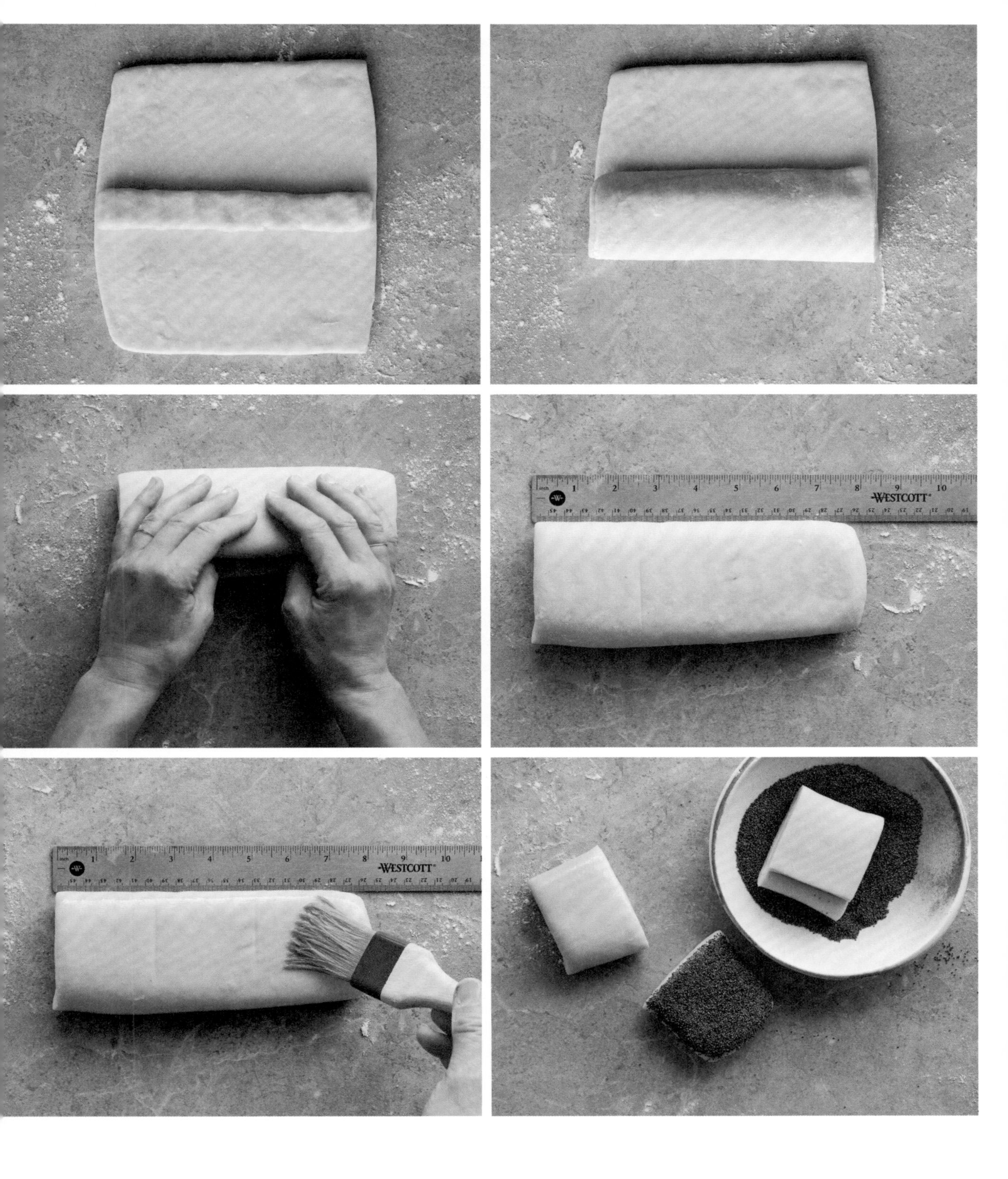
WESTCOTT
WESTCOTT

SEEDED SAVORY PASTRIES

Grovbirkes

Grovbirkes are the savory cousin of Tebirkes (page 149). They are made of the same dough and shaped in exactly the same manner, minus the sweet almond paste filling, and covered in a variety of seeds rather than just poppy seeds. I adore both, but the truth is that as much as I love me a tebirkes, I actually eat grovbirkes more often because they're still rich but not quite as decadent. These are what we use as a bun when we make the Grovbirkes Sandwich (page 184). MAKES 10 GROVBIRKES

Danish Dough (page 135)

Flour for dusting

1 egg

3 tablespoons sunflower seeds

1 tablespoon flax seeds

1 tablespoon sesame seeds

1 tablespoon pumpkin seeds

1 tablespoon poppy seeds

MAKE THE DOUGH

Follow the directions on page 135, up to and including fold no. 3. The dough should be chilled and ready to use.

Line two 13 by 18-inch (33 by 46 cm) baking trays with parchment paper.

Lightly dust a work surface with flour. Position the dough on a work surface with one of the short (6-inch/15 cm) ends close to you, parallel to the edge of the work surface. Roll the dough out, using vertical (up and down) motions, into a 9 by 25-inch (23 by 63 cm) strip, gently tugging and pinching at the corners to square them off as best you can. Reposition the strip of dough horizontally so that the long end is parallel with the edge of your work space.

Imagine the long strip being divided into thirds vertically, and then fold the bottom third of the dough up onto the middle third and pat it down. Then fold the top third of the dough down, overlapping the bottom piece by about 1 inch (2.5 cm). Again, pinch and pull at the corners to make them come as close to a 90-degree angle as possible. Flip the strip over, seam side down. Super gently (using only the weight of the rolling pin), flatten it ever so slightly. Using a dry pastry brush, brush off any excess flour (otherwise the flour will affect how well the seed mix adheres to the pastry).

In a small bowl, whisk the egg with a fork. Using the same pastry brush, lightly brush the top of the entire strip with the egg wash.

Using a chef's knife, make ten shallow cuts at 2½-inch (6 cm) intervals. Then cut the strip into slices using the marks as your guide.

In a shallow bowl or container, combine the sunflower, flax, sesame, pumpkin, and poppy seeds and stir to incorporate. Dip each slice, egg wash side down, into the seeds. Press gently to make them adhere and then place the grovbirkes, seeded side up, onto the prepared baking trays. You should have five grovbirkes, evenly spaced, per baking tray.

PROOF THE GROVBIRKES

Cover the grovbirkes with a kitchen towel and set them in a warm and draft-free area until they are noticeably puffier, slightly dry looking, and the impression of a fingerprint is slow to fill in, 1 to 2 hours, depending on the temperature of your kitchen. For an alternate method that takes less time but requires a more watchful eye, see "Proofing Dough" on page 36.

When the grovbirkes are sufficiently proofed, preheat the oven to 375°F (190°C).

Bake for 25 to 30 minutes, rotating the baking trays halfway through from top to bottom and front to back, until the pastry looks dark golden brown and the seeds are toasted. These are best eaten warm or on the day they are baked. If you have some left over, store them in an airtight container until ready to enjoy, then heat them for 5 to 10 minutes in a preheated 350°F (175°C) oven.

APPLE AND PASTRY CREAM STRIP

Æblekringle

A stunning, large-format pastry like this is meant for sharing. Tucked inside the flaky braid, rich vanilla-flecked pastry cream and tart apple compote meld together. While this recipe does contain several components, you can make your pastry cream, compote, and danish dough ahead of time and assemble everything on the day it is baked. If you don't have time to make an apple compote, this braid is also delicious made with pastry cream and black currant or lingonberry jam. (The one from Ikea is not bad.) MAKES ONE 17-INCH (43 CM) BRAIDED PASTRY (ENOUGH FOR 10 TO 12 SERVINGS)

Danish Dough (page 135)

Pastry cream (see page 92)

Apple compote

3 apples (450 g), peeled, cored, and cut into 1-inch (2.5 cm) dice (I like a tart apple, like Honeycrisp or Pink Lady)

½ cup (100 g) sugar

½ cup (118 g) water

Zest and juice of 1 lemon

2 cinnamon sticks

1 vanilla bean, split lengthwise

Kosher salt

To finish

Flour for dusting

1 egg

3 tablespoons cardamom sugar (see page 77)

Vanilla ice cream for serving (optional)

MAKE THE DOUGH

Follow the directions on page 135, up to and including fold no. 3. The dough should be chilled and ready to use.

MAKE THE PASTRY CREAM

Follow the pastry cream recipe in Summer Strawberry Tart on page 92. It should be chilled and ready to use.

MAKE THE COMPOTE

In a medium pot, add the apples, sugar, water, lemon zest and juice, and cinnamon sticks. Scrape in the seeds from the vanilla bean and stir everything together. Bring the mixture to a simmer over medium heat and allow the compote to cook for 10 to 15 minutes, until much of the liquid has evaporated and the apples are slightly translucent but still holding their shape. Stir occasionally and monitor the liquid level so that it does not dry out. You don't want this to turn into a complete mush, especially as the apples will continue to cook and soften in the oven. Taste and add up to ½ teaspoon of salt. Transfer the mixture to a bowl, cool completely, and chill in the refrigerator until ready to use.

Lightly dust a work surface with flour. Position the dough on the work surface with one of the short (6-inch/15 cm) ends close to you, parallel to the edge of the work surface. Roll the dough out, using vertical (up and down) motions, into an 11 by 17-inch (28 by 43 cm) rectangle, gently tugging and pinching at the corners to square them off as best you can.

CONTINUED

Transfer the rectangle of dough to a sheet of parchment paper. Position it with one long (17-inch/43 cm) end closest to you, parallel to the edge of your work surface. Using a ruler, divide the rectangle horizontally into thirds, measuring two lines, each 3 inches (7.5 cm) from the upper and lower edges of the rectangle. Use the edge of your ruler to gently make shallow indents on the dough as place markers. Do not cut through the pastry yet! You should have a 3 by 17-inch (7.5 by 43 cm) vertical strip, followed by a 5 by 17-inch (12.5 by 43 cm) center section, followed by one more 3 by 17-inch (7.5 by 43 cm) vertical strip.

Now pivot the dough on the parchment paper 90 degrees so that it's facing you lengthwise, with one of the short (11-inch/28 cm) ends parallel to the edge of your work surface. You are going to cut 1-inch (2.5 cm) strips into both the left and right portions of the dough (the ones measuring 3 by 17 inches/7.5 by 43 cm), leaving the middle portion uncut. Again use your ruler to gently make shallow indents to mark the dough at 1-inch (2.5 cm) intervals along both sides of the strip. You should have seventeen 1-inch (2.5 cm) strips both to the left and right of the uncut center portion of the dough. Once you've marked them, cut through them with a chef's knife, being sure to leave the center of the dough uncut where the fillings will go. (See photographs for guidance.) Now slide the dough onto a baking tray, using the parchment paper to help ease this transfer. You will bake it on this same piece of parchment paper, so don't discard it.

Spread the pastry cream across the uncut center of the dough, using an offset spatula to spread it as evenly as possible across the entire surface.

Use a slotted spoon to disperse the apple compote evenly over the pastry cream, leaving behind as much liquid as possible, which could make your pastry soggy and hard to seal while braiding. You may or may not use all of the apple compote. You want the compote to cover the entire center section of the dough, but don't heap it, or the braid won't cover the filling.

Position the baking tray so that the pastry is facing you vertically, with one of the short ends parallel to the edge of the work surface. Cut away the top and bottom strips from the left and right sides of the dough, and discard them. This will leave fifteen strips on either side of the compote and cream covered center. Where you have removed the top and bottom

strips, there will be 1-inch (2.5 cm) flaps. Fold them over the filling to reduce seepage during baking. Pull one strip of dough across the filling, at a slight downward diagonal. Then pull the same strip across the filling from the other side, alternating between left and right to create a pattern that resembles a braid or shoelaces on a sneaker. There may be a slight gap at the end of a strip that doesn't completely enclose the filling, but no worries. The next strip pulled from the alternate side will cover the gap left by the previous strip. As you reach the end, flip the end flap (created by removing the strips in the beginning) over the filling and finish the "braid" over the flap to prevent the filling from oozing out of the end during baking. The last strips can be gently tucked under the butt end of the kringle.

In a small bowl, whisk the egg with a fork. Using a pastry brush, lightly brush the entire surface of the braid with the egg wash and then sprinkle the cardamom sugar over top.

PROOF THE KRINGLE

Cover the kringle with a kitchen towel and set them in a warm and draft-free area until it is noticeably puffier, slightly dry looking, and the impression of a fingerprint is slow to fill in, 1 to 2 hours, depending on the temperature of your kitchen. For an alternate method that takes less time but requires a more watchful eye, see "Proofing Dough" on page 36.

When the kringle is sufficiently proofed, preheat the oven to 375°F (190°C).

Bake for 40 to 45 minutes, rotating the tray halfway through, until the pastry looks dark golden brown. Serve it in thick slices, ideally topped with vanilla ice cream. This pastry is best eaten warm or on the day it is baked. If you have some left over, store it in an airtight container until ready to enjoy, then heat it for 5 to 10 minutes in a preheated 350°F (175°C) oven.

SEEDED HAVARTI TWISTS

Frøsnapper

These twists are made by encrusting the bottom of a strip of danish dough in poppy seeds and the top in sesame seeds. Twisted, they achieve a striped barbershop-pole effect. I sandwich a generous quantity of grated Havarti cheese into my folded pastry, making these crisp and chewy twists irresistibly buttery and cheesy at the same time. Feel free to substitute goat cheese, aged Gouda, or any other cheese that you love. They always fly off our bakery shelves when we sell them at Kantine. If it's warm in your kitchen while you are shaping these, work swiftly. If your dough is getting warm and sticky from being handled, just put it back in the refrigerator for twenty minutes to firm up again, and you'll be good to go.

If you want to make a sweet version of these, you can omit the cheese and instead spread a thick layer of the same almond filling used in tebirkes (page 149). Keep the gorgeous poppy and sesame seeds! **MAKES 16 TWISTS**

Danish Dough (page 135)

Flour for dusting

8 ounces (225 g) grated Havarti cheese

Pinch of freshly ground black pepper

To finish

1 egg

3 tablespoons poppy seeds

3 tablespoons sesame seeds

MAKE THE DOUGH

Follow the directions on page 135, up to and including fold no. 3. The dough should be chilled and ready to use.

Line two 13 by 18-inch (33 by 46 cm) baking trays with parchment paper.

Lightly dust a work surface with flour. Position the dough on the work surface with one of the short (6-inch/15 cm) ends close to you, parallel to the edge of the work surface. Roll the dough out, using vertical (up and down) motions, into an 8 by 24-inch (20 by 60 cm) strip, gently tugging and pinching at the corners to square them off as best you can. Rotate it 90 degrees so that it is now positioned horizontally, with one of the long (24-inch/60 cm) ends closest to you, parallel to the edge of the work surface.

Cut the strip in half down the middle, making two rectangles that measure 8 by 12 inches (20 by 30 cm) each. This will make them easier to work with.

Positioned each rectangle vertically with the short (8-inch/20 cm) end closest to you, parallel to the edge of the work surface.

Scatter 4 ounces (113 g) of the Havarti on the lower half of each rectangle, followed by a grind of pepper.

For each rectangle, fold the top half of the dough over the cheese and pat it down. Give the dough a quick roll with the rolling pin so that it's even and not noticeably fatter or thinner in any parts. Trim off any

uneven edges with a chef's knife. Roll them both out slightly so that each rectangle measures about 6 by 8 inches (15 by 20 cm).

In a small bowl, whisk the egg with a fork.

Using a dry pastry brush, brush off any excess flour (otherwise the flour will affect how well the seeds adhere to the pastry). Using a different pastry brush, lightly brush the entire surface of each rectangle with the egg wash. Scatter both with the poppy seeds, patting them down to make sure that they stick. Flip both rectangles of dough over. Again, using the dry pastry brush, brush off any excess flour and then brush the entire surface of each with the egg wash, using the wet pastry brush. Scatter this side with the sesame seeds, patting them down to make sure that they stick.

With a ruler and a chef's knife, measure and cut each rectangle into eight horizontal 1-inch (2.5 cm) strips. You will have sixteen strips total.

With one hand, pinch one end of one strip to hold it in place and with your other hand, twist twice. You should see a cool barbershop swirl emerge with both kinds of seeds visible in alternating stripes. Place the twist on one of the prepared baking trays and repeat with the remaining strips of dough. You should have eight twists per tray, evenly spaced.

PROOF THE TWISTS

Cover the shaped pastry with a kitchen towel and set them in a warm and draft-free area until they are noticeably puffier, slightly dry looking, and the impression of a fingerprint is slow to fill in, 1 to 2 hours, depending on the temperature of your kitchen. For an alternate method that takes less time but requires a more watchful eye, see "Proofing Dough" on page 36.

When the twists are sufficiently proofed, preheat the oven to 375°F (190°C).

Bake for 40 to 45 minutes, rotating the baking trays halfway through from top to bottom and front to back, until the pastry looks dark golden brown and the seeds are toasted. These are best enjoyed warm or on the day they are baked. If you have some left over, store them in an airtight container until ready to enjoy, then heat them for 5 to 10 minutes in a preheated 350°F (175°C) oven.

HERBED GOAT CHEESE, CARAMELIZED ONION, AND GOLDEN POTATO DANISH

Scandinavian potatoes are one of the foods I miss most when I'm in the United States. Sweet and tender, I could easily pop them in my mouth like bonbons. Here in Northern California, I buy Bintje potatoes grown by Full Belly Farm, which take the cake as the best stateside substitute I've found so far. If you can't get your hands on those, opt for small yellow or new potatoes. For these danishes, the new potatoes are sliced and shingled atop goat cheese blended with fresh herbs. I recommend having your potatoes boiled, cooled, and ready to go when you take the danish dough out of the refrigerator. MAKES 12 DANISHES

Danish Dough (page 135)

Flour for dusting

2 tablespoons unsalted butter

3 to 4 medium onions, chopped

10½ ounces (287 g) soft goat cheese

4 tablespoons sliced fresh chives or other chopped fresh herb

Olive oil

1 egg

10 to 12 new or small yellow potatoes, boiled to fork-tender and cooled (see Note)

To finish

Kosher salt and freshly ground black pepper

A few different fresh herbs for garnish

MAKE THE DOUGH

Follow the directions on page 135, up to and including fold no. 3. The dough should be chilled and ready to use.

Line two 13 by 18-inch (33 by 46 cm) baking trays with parchment paper.

Lightly dust a work surface with flour and then roll the book of dough into a 8 by 18-inch (20 by 46 cm) rectangle, gently tugging and pinching at the corners to square them off as best you can. Reposition it horizontally with one long (18-inch/46 cm) end closest to you, parallel to the edge of the work surface. Trim off the edges to neaten the corners, then measure it again. Roll it out slightly if needed to return to the original dimensions. Using a ruler and a chef's knife, measure and cut six vertical 3-inch (7.5 cm) strips. Then cut each of the strips in half at the midpoint, yielding twelve rectangles of dough measuring approximately 4 by 3 inches (10 by 7.5 cm) each. Place six rectangles of dough on each of the prepared trays.

PROOF THE DANISH

Cover the danishes with a kitchen towel and set them in a warm and draft-free area until they are noticeably puffier, slightly dry looking, and the impression of a fingerprint is slow to fill in, 1 to 2 hours, depending on the temperature of your kitchen. For an alternate method that takes less time but requires a more watchful eye, see "Proofing Dough" on page 36.

While the danishes are proofing, caramelize the onions. In a large skillet over medium heat, melt the butter. Add the onions and sauté them for 15 to 20 minutes, stirring occasionally, until dark golden brown. Transfer the onions to a bowl to cool.

CONTINUED

In the bowl of a stand mixer fitted with the paddle attachment, combine the goat cheese, 3 tablespoons of the chives, and 1 tablespoon olive oil and mix on medium until well incorporated.

In a small bowl, whisk the egg with a fork. When the danishes are sufficiently proofed, use a pastry brush to lightly coat the entire surface of each danish with the egg wash.

Preheat the oven to 375°F (190°C).

Using the back of a spoon or an offset spatula, make a shallow depression in the center of each rectangle. Don't stress out about the exact shape of it.

Place a heaping tablespoon of the goat cheese mixture in the center of each rectangle and gently spread it out with an offset spatula, leaving a ½-inch (1 cm) border. Evenly distribute the caramelized onions over the cheese. Cut the potatoes into ¼-inch-thick (6 mm) slices and place them on top of the onions in a slightly overlapping shingled pattern. You should be able to fit four or five slices (roughly the equivalent of 1 small potato) per danish. Sprinkle with salt and pepper and drizzle very lightly with the oil.

Bake for 30 to 35 minutes, rotating the baking trays halfway through from top to bottom and front to back, until the pastry looks dark golden brown and the potatoes are also lightly browned. Garnish with the remaining 1 tablespoon chives and other fresh herbs right before serving. These danishes are best eaten warm or on the day they are baked. If you have some left over, store them in an airtight container until ready to enjoy, then heat them for 5 to 10 minutes in a preheated 350°F (175°C) oven.

NOTE To boil the potatoes, place them (skin on) in a medium pot and completely cover them with water. Salt the water heavily, 2 tablespoons of salt per cup of water. Bring to a boil over medium-high heat. Decrease the heat and let the potatoes simmer for about 15 minutes (time will vary slightly depending on the size of the potatoes), until fork-tender. Transfer them to a colander to drain and cool completely.

RISE AND SHINE

I am an early-morning person, and the first thing I think about when I wake up is what I can eat for breakfast. I love breakfast because it's the first ritual of the day, and it means I have a whole new day ahead of me. In my opinion, there are too few daytime restaurants out there, especially ones that focus on serving brunch during the week. Not everyone has a nine-to-five job and is off on the weekend. Why shouldn't you treat yourself to a Tuesday-morning brunch, if you can? I wanted Kantine to be a breakfast and lunch restaurant, allowing me to take advantage of my favorite time of day and share my favorite Scandinavian foods with others.

A typical Scandinavian breakfast is usually a bowl of yogurt or porridge, or buttered rye bread with cheese or meat. On the weekends, people give the first meal of the day more attention. Often this means a trip to a favorite bakery or a leisurely brunch at a restaurant. At Kantine, we have a brunch board, where people select five or seven items out of an array of possibilities on the menu. Every brunch board comes with either Danish rye bread or flatbread. Here I've provided some of our most beloved brunch board items, like the Runny Egg with Spinach Cream (page 191) and Citrus Salad with Mint Tarragon Sugar (page 189).

In Danish, you use the verb "to bake" for pancakes and waffles, even though these are made on the stovetop or in a waffle iron, which is why I decided to include these recipes in a baking cookbook. I make both my Soft Flatbread (page 173) and Lefse (page 171) flatbreads in a regular cast-iron pan. I've also included a recipe for waffles (page 179), perfumed with cardamom, and given a pleasing tartness thanks to the kefir in the batter.

Making a special breakfast doesn't have to be complicated. Garnishes are an easy way to add zing to an everyday breakfast. Tear a few mint leaves to mix in with fresh fruit, sprinkle dried thyme onto good-quality butter, or get out your jar of cardamom sugar (see page 77) to sprinkle over oatmeal or porridge. These little touches make food stand out and show that care was put into it, and they don't need to be reserved for others. Breakfast can be part of a self-care routine, setting you up for a great day, whether it's the weekend or not.

POTATO FLATBREAD

Lefse

Lefser (lefse in the singular) are traditional flatbreads from Norway made from flour, butter, cream, and sometimes potatoes. Some people call them "Norwegian pancakes," but they are closer to a tortilla in their versatility. In Norway, you might just as easily find lefser on the table at the reception for a fancy wedding as sold at gas stations as a convenient snack. While they are frequently served like a dinner roll—a humble starch used to sop up the juices of a meal—they can also be eaten as a sweet treat, slathered with butter, sprinkled liberally with sugar, and rolled up. As you can imagine, kids tend to prefer the latter.

In Norway, lefser are often featured at holiday meals, a tradition that has been passed down in Norwegian American households, many of which are in possession of a special lefse pan and notched rolling pin (see page 30). You can definitely make them without these supplies, however. This recipe calls for potatoes to be mashed with butter and cream and chilled overnight before flour is added to form a dough that gets rolled into thin disks and cooked in a hot skillet. If you happen to have leftover mashed potatoes (say, after Thanksgiving), this would be a fun way to use them up. My favorite way to eat lefser is spread with herbed cream cheese and topped with gravlax or smoked trout, pickled red onions, capers, and fresh dill.

MAKES TEN 8-INCH (20 CM) FLATBREADS

2½ pounds (1.1 kg) Yukon Gold or other creamer potatoes, peeled and cut into 1-inch (2.5 cm) chunks

½ cup (113 g) unsalted butter, at room temperature, plus more as needed

½ cup (113 g) heavy cream

2½ teaspoons kosher salt

3 cups (384 g) all-purpose flour, plus more for dusting

Place the potatoes in a large saucepan and cover them with water. Bring the water to a gentle boil over medium-high heat and cook for 10 to 12 minutes, until the potatoes are tender. Drain the potatoes and transfer them to a large bowl, adding the butter while the potatoes are still hot, so that it melts. Using a potato masher, ricer, or dinner fork, mash them as thoroughly as you can. Add the cream and 2 teaspoons of the salt and continue mixing until the potatoes are smooth and creamy. Taste them and add the remaining ½ teaspoon salt, if desired. Transfer the potatoes to an airtight container and refrigerate them overnight.

When you are ready to make the lefser, liberally dust a work surface with flour. Begin adding the flour to the bowl with the chilled mashed potatoes, 1 cup (128 g) at a time, until it forms a soft and shaggy dough. You can start mixing this dough with a wooden spoon but eventually you will need to turn the dough out onto the work surface and put some muscle into it to crush the potato chunks and knead it into a smooth ball. Roll the dough into a thick log and then divide it into ten portions. Roll each portion into a ball and cover them with a clean kitchen towel.

CONTINUED

Set an ungreased cast-iron pan (or lefse pan, if you have one) over medium-high heat, letting it heat up for a few minutes. You need the pan to be very hot to create the dark spots that characteristically freckle lefser.

With a bench scraper, clean any doughy residue off the work surface where you rolled the balls of dough, then liberally dust it with more flour before you start rolling out the first ball, as this is a very sticky dough.

When rolling out the dough, follow the "air hockey" method (see page 36). Be sure to repeatedly slide a bench scraper under the rolled-out dough, dusting more flour onto the work surface beneath it as needed and flipping it as you work. Don't worry about the amount of flour used to roll out the lefser; any excess will be brushed off prior to baking. While rolling, apply soft and even pressure and regularly check to make sure that you can always lift the dough off the work surface. With all of this in mind, roll out the first ball of dough to about 8 inches (20 cm) in diameter.

When your lefse is as thin as you can make it, brush off any excess flour with a dry pastry brush. If you have a notched rolling pin, roll it once over the surface of your dough. If not, prick the surface of the flattened dough all over (about thirty-five times) with the tines of a fork. Gently roll it over and around your rolling pin and carry it that way to the stove, carefully unfurling it directly into the hot pan.

Cook your lefse for 1 to 2 minutes on each side, until speckled with golden brown spots. While each lefse is cooking, roll out the next one to have ready. If you have two cast-iron pans, you could heat both and cook two lefser at once.

Transfer each cooked lefse to a plate, covering the pile with a clean kitchen towel while you continue to roll out and cook the remaining balls of dough. If the lefser start to stick to the pan, add a bit of butter.

Lefser are typically served at room temperature, spread with savory or sweet toppings. My favorite way to eat them is to smear them with butter, sprinkle with cardamom sugar and roll them up (see the photograph on page 170). It just works! I think they are best served fresh on the day they are made, but they can be stored in an airtight container in the refrigerator for up to 1 week. Just make sure to place a sheet of parchment paper between each lefse before storing.

SOFT FLATBREAD

Tunnbröd

A quartet of freshly ground caraway, coriander, fennel, and anise seeds gives these soft Swedish flatbreads an enticing aroma as well as taste. They're ever so slightly sweet, making them an excellent counterpoint to cured meat or salty cheeses. In Sweden, these flatbreads are sometimes wrapped around a hot dog instead of a bun. While Scandinavia is all about minimalism, there are exceptions to every rule. I was once handed a flatbread wrapped around not one but two hot dogs, hot mashed potatoes, and creamy shrimp salad! It's what Swedes call tunnbrödsrulle, and it was scrumptious! **MAKES TWELVE 8-INCH (20 CM) FLATBREADS**

Pre-ferment

- 1 cup (128 g) all-purpose flour
- 1 cup (120 g) rye flour
- 1 cup (240 g) whole milk
- 1 heaping teaspoon active dry yeast

Main dough

- 1 cup (240 g) whole milk
- 6 tablespoons (83 g) unsalted butter
- ⅓ cup (100 g) light corn syrup
- 1 teaspoon anise seeds
- 1 teaspoon fennel seeds
- 1 teaspoon coriander seeds
- 1 teaspoon caraway seeds
- 4 cups (512 g) all-purpose flour, plus more for dusting
- 1 teaspoon kosher salt
- ½ heaping teaspoon baking soda

MAKE THE PRE-FERMENT

In the bowl of a stand mixer, combine the all-purpose flour, rye flour, milk, and yeast and whisk. Cover the bowl with a clean kitchen towel and let it rest in a warm place for 30 minutes.

WHILE THE PRE-FERMENT IS RESTING, BEGIN THE MAIN DOUGH

In a small saucepan, heat the milk over medium heat to about 110°F (43°C), or until it starts to bubble around the edges of the pan. Do not bring it to a full boil. Remove it from the stove and add the butter and corn syrup.

In a spice grinder or clean coffee grinder, grind the anise, fennel, coriander, and caraway seeds to a fine powder. (Blend them all together, as these are such small quantities that it would be difficult otherwise.)

When the pre-ferment is ready, add the flour, salt, and baking soda to the mixer bowl.

Stir the milk mixture to make sure that the corn syrup and butter have melted into it. Test the temperature with your fingertip, making sure it's not too hot (120°F/49°C, max), as too high of a temperature will kill the yeast, resulting in extremely flat flatbread.

Add the ground spices to the bowl, followed by the milk mixture. Using the dough hook attachment, knead the dough for about 5 minutes, until the dough is smooth, silky, and elastic. Cover it again with the kitchen towel and let it rise for 1 hour.

CONTINUED

Divide the dough into twelve balls. To form the buns, hold your hand in a relaxed claw shape, gently curling your fingers over a ball of dough. While placing very light pressure on the ball, rub your wrist and fingertips repeatedly in a circular motion against the work surface, holding the dough loosely as you feel it become rounder and smoother. Repeat this for all of the balls of dough. Cover the balls with the kitchen towel so that they don't dry out.

Lightly dust a work surface with flour. Using a floured rolling pin, roll one of the dough balls until it forms a flattened circle, about 8 inches (20 cm) across. Brush off the excess flour. If you have a notched rolling pin (see page 30), roll it once over the surface of your flatbread. If not, prick the surface of the flattened dough all over (about thirty-five times) with the tines of a fork.

Immediately set an ungreased cast-iron pan over medium-high heat. When the pan is hot, place the notched flatbread in the pan. Once the bread has slightly puffed in the pan and has brown flecks on the underside, flip it using a spatula, and cook for 2 minutes more. While the flatbread is cooking, roll out the next dough ball.

The flatbread will puff slightly as you cook it and get flecks on both sides. The goal is to cook it completely but still maintain a soft and pliable texture, similar to a pita. Once the flatbread is done cooking, remove it from the pan and place it on a rack to cool. (If you put it on a counter or plate, it will get sweaty.) Continue to roll the remaining balls of dough and cook each one, placing it on top of the finished flatbreads in a growing stack. You don't have to worry about these getting sweaty, as the steaminess gets absorbed by the stack.

These flatbreads are best enjoyed warm, but they can also be stored in an airtight container for 1 day at room temperature or for several days in the refrigerator. If you refrigerate them, give each one a quick toast before eating.

RYE CRISPBREAD

Knäckebröd

Rye crispbreads, a staple food in Sweden, are large and extremely crisp crackers (thus the name!) with a hole in the center that are often eaten with toppings as a snack or part of breakfast or lunch. The reason for that hole dates back to the olden days when people would thread the crispy disks onto a wooden dowel near the ceiling, a place where they could stay dry and out of the way until needed. Knäckebröd retain their signature crispiness for a long time, so go ahead and make a large batch if you like them as they won't soon go stale. I love the savory flavor of the added caraway seeds combined with butter and cheese. MAKES FOUR 8-INCH (20 CM) CRISPBREADS

- 1 teaspoon active dry yeast
- ½ cup (118 g) lukewarm water
- 1½ cups (180 g) coarse rye flour, plus more as needed
- 1½ teaspoons unsalted butter, at room temperature
- 1 teaspoon caraway seeds, crushed
- ½ teaspoon kosher salt
- Flaked salt for garnish

In a medium bowl, stir the yeast and water together until the yeast has dissolved. Let the mixture stand at room temperature for 10 minutes.

Stir in the rye flour, butter, ½ teaspoon of the caraway seeds, and the kosher salt. The dough may seem a bit wet, but that can be adjusted later. Once it starts to form a ball, use your fingers to finish mixing. Because this is made with rye flour, it will be a sticky dough.

Lightly dust a work surface with rye flour. Divide the dough into four portions of approximately 75 g each (you should have about 300 g of dough total). Form each portion into a ball, cover them with a clean kitchen towel, and let them rest for 45 minutes.

After about 30 minutes, line two 13 by 18-inch (33 by 46 cm) baking trays with parchment paper, arrange two racks in the upper and lower thirds of the oven, and preheat the oven to 325°F (165°C).

With a bench scraper, clean any doughy residue off the work surface where you divided your dough and then lightly dust it again with rye flour. Using a floured rolling pin, roll one of the balls of dough into a circle, about 8 inches (20 cm) in diameter and very thin. If the dough seems too sticky to handle, be liberal with adding more rye flour. You definitely want to use the "air hockey" method of rolling out dough here (see page 36). This means rolling the dough gently, loosening and lifting it up, and adding more flour to your work surface as you go. Once your dough is large enough, brush off any excess flour with a dry pastry brush.

CONTINUED

Gently roll it over and around your rolling pin and carry it to one of the prepared baking trays. Unfurl it onto the tray. If you have a notched rolling pin (see page 30), roll it once over the surface of the dough. If not, prick the surface of the dough all over (about thirty times) with the tines of a fork. Repeat this with the remaining three balls of dough. You should have two crispbreads per baking tray.

To create the traditional hole in the center of each round of dough, punch a 2-inch (5 cm) hole in the middle using a cookie cutter or shot glass, discarding the small circle of dough. Cut off any ruffled edges to round the crispbreads out and sprinkle a bit of water on the surface, followed by a dash of the flaked salt and the remaining ½ teaspoon caraway seeds.

Bake for 20 to 25 minutes, rotating the baking trays halfway through from top to bottom and front to back, until lightly golden brown and lifting up from the parchment paper. The crispbreads will continue to crisp up after they cool. Transfer them to a rack to cool completely before serving.

Store the rye crispbreads in an airtight container, where they will stay fresh for at least 3 weeks. If they do not seem quite crisp enough, return them to a preheated 325°F (165°C) oven for 4 to 5 minutes.

WAFFLES WITH KEFIR AND CARDAMOM

Vafler med Kefir og Kardemomme

This recipe came from my Norwegian friend Tonje Vetletseter. She got the recipe from her mother, and they are some of the best waffles I've ever tasted (which is saying a lot since we eat a lot of waffles in our house). Norwegian waffles are thin and crispy at the edges thanks to the special waffle iron (see page 33). The batter is subtly tangy from kefir and possesses a distinctly Scandinavian taste from a full teaspoon of cardamom. For perfectly crisp, golden edges, be sure to turn your waffle iron on as soon as you start making your batter. For crispy waffles, preheat for fifteen minutes. You can pour this batter into a Belgian waffle iron, but the texture and yield will be different. MAKES 10 TO 12 WAFFLES

- 4 eggs
- ½ cup (100 g) granulated sugar
- 2 cups (256 g) all-purpose flour
- 1 teaspoon freshly ground decorticated cardamom (see page 21)
- ½ teaspoon baking soda
- ½ teaspoon kosher salt
- 2 cups (480 g) plain whole-milk kefir
- 7 tablespoons (100 g) unsalted butter, melted, plus more for greasing

To finish

- 1 cup (226 g) heavy cream
- 3 tablespoons powdered sugar
- Jam or fresh fruit for serving

Preheat a waffle iron on high heat for 15 minutes while you prepare the batter.

In the bowl of a stand mixer fitted with the whisk attachment, beat the eggs and granulated sugar on medium until the mixture has thickened and turned a pale yellow, 2 to 3 minutes.

In a medium bowl, whisk together the flour, cardamom, baking soda, and salt.

Add the flour mixture and the kefir to the egg mixture, and mix on low until everything is well incorporated, 1 to 2 minutes. Stir in the melted butter. Let the batter sit until the waffle iron finishes preheating.

Butter the waffle iron before cooking the first waffle. You probably won't need to butter it after that. Using a ladle, pour about ½ cup (115 g) of the batter onto the hot waffle iron and close the lid. Cook for about 6 minutes per waffle, checking occasionally to see how brown it is. The waffle should be dark gold at the edges. Place the waffle on a plate and repeat with the remaining batter.

WHILE WAFFLES ARE COOKING, MAKE THE WHIPPED CREAM

In the bowl of a stand mixer fitted with the whisk attachment, whip the cream on medium until soft peaks form (see page 37). Add the powdered sugar and whip again.

Serve the waffles immediately with the whipped cream and jam.

RYE AND BEER PANCAKES
Rug Pandekager

Scandinavian pancakes look similar to French crepes, but they are lighter and chewier thanks to more eggs and less flour. Beer gives the batter a malted earthiness. When served with lightly sweetened whipped cream and berry compote, the results are heavenly. On the rare occasion when there are leftovers, they make a quick and easy snack spread with butter, sprinkled with cardamom sugar (see page 77), and rolled up. I suggest making the berry compote and whipping the cream before cooking the pancakes, so that they are ready to serve with the hot pancakes.

MAKES 8 TO 10 PANCAKES

- ⅔ cup (70 g) cake flour
- ¾ cup (85 g) rye flour
- ¼ teaspoon kosher salt
- 4 eggs
- 1 cup (240 g) whole milk
- 2 tablespoons unsalted butter, melted, plus more for greasing
- 1 cup (237 g) beer (pilsner or pale ale)
- 1 cup (226 g) heavy cream
- 3 tablespoons powdered sugar
- Berry compote (see box) or fresh fruit, for serving

In a medium bowl, whisk the cake flour, rye flour, and salt until well combined.

In a separate medium bowl, whisk the eggs, milk, and melted butter until frothy. Add the flour mixture and whisk until well incorporated and no floury lumps remain. Add the beer and whisk for 1 minute more. Set aside.

In the bowl of a stand mixer fitted with the whisk attachment or in a large bowl with a handheld mixer, whip the cream on medium until soft peaks form (see page 37). Add the powdered sugar and whip again.

Lightly butter a medium nonstick skillet or crepe pan and set it over medium heat. The batter is buttery enough that you may not need to butter the pan again for the remaining pancakes. Using a ladle, drop about ⅔ cup (65 g) of the batter onto the pan, lifting and swirling the pan to cover the surface thinly. Let the pancake cook for 2 minutes, until the surface looks dry and the edges are browned and lifting away from the pan. Flip it and let it cook on the other side for 1 minute more. Place the pancake on a plate and repeat with the remaining batter, stacking the pancakes as you go. Serve immediately with bowls of sweetened whipped cream and berry compote.

BERRY COMPOTE

In a medium saucepan, combine the blackberries, sugar, lemon juice, and water over low heat. Using a wooden spoon, crush the berries against the side of the pot until the sugar dissolves. Increase the heat to medium-high and simmer for 2 minutes to thicken. Stir in the raspberries. Cook for 2 minutes more, then remove from the heat and transfer to a bowl. Serve hot or cold. Store in an airtight container in the refrigerator for up to 5 days.

- 1 cup (150 g) fresh blackberries
- ¼ cup (50 g) sugar
- 1 teaspoon fresh lemon juice
- 1 tablespoon water
- 1 cup (150 g) frozen raspberries

RYE AND OAT GRANOLA

At Kantine, we always have an abundance of scraps and ends of our sprouted rye bread since you can't serve the heel or uneven pieces to customers. This granola is the perfect way to use those leftover bread scraps. Breadcrumbs and oats form the base, mixed with seeds and coated in a blend of honey and melted butter before it's all baked to a crisp. The result is wholesome yet addictive, filling, and extremely crunchy. The texture and taste remind me slightly of Grape-Nuts but so much better! This granola makes a great crunchy topping for yogurt or oatmeal. For something extra special, top off your bowl of granola with a tablespoon of fresh mint tarragon sugar (see page 189).

I realize it could take you some time to save enough heels and pieces of bread to yield six cups of crumbs. So freeze your scraps as you go along until you reach your goal or double the recipe next time, yielding one for eating and the other exclusively for granola. Just make sure that you have two bread pans to proof them simultaneously. **MAKES ABOUT 8 CUPS**

- 4¾ cups (500 g) torn or cubed fresh or stale Sprouted Rye Bread (page 198)
- 2 cups (225 g) rolled oats
- 1 cup (100 g) sunflower seeds
- ⅔ cup (100 g) pumpkin seeds
- 1 tablespoon kosher salt
- ½ cup (113 g) unsalted butter
- 1 cup (200 g) honey
- ½ cup (100 g) packed light brown sugar

Line two 13 by 18-inch (33 by 46 cm) baking trays with parchment paper. Arrange two racks in the upper and lower thirds of the oven and preheat the oven to 325°F (165°C).

Add half of the bread to a food processor and pulse until it forms large crumbs (about the same size as the rolled oats). Transfer them to a large bowl and repeat with the remaining bread. Then add the oats, sunflower seeds, pumpkin seeds, and salt to the bowl with the breadcrumbs.

In a medium saucepan over medium-high heat, melt the butter and then add the honey and brown sugar. Stir until combined. Add the butter mixture to the breadcrumb mixture and stir until everything is uniformly coated.

Spread the mixture onto the prepared baking trays, evenly dividing it and spreading it as thinly as possible from edge to edge.

Bake for 35 to 40 minutes, rotating the baking trays halfway through from top to bottom and front to back and stirring every 10 minutes, until the granola is a dark brown color. You want to bake it at this low temperature so that the oats and seeds don't burn before they have a chance to dry out and get crisp. Stirring it periodically ensures that all the oats and breadcrumbs get exposed to the heat evenly.

Let the granola cool completely before transferring it to an airtight container, or else it will lose its crunch. It will keep fresh for up to 2 weeks.

THE GROVBIRKES SANDWICH

At Kantine, our breakfast sandwich comes on a grovbirkes, made with flaky danish dough encrusted in seeds. I was initially reluctant to have a breakfast sandwich on the menu because it's not a typical Scandinavian thing, and I was trying to stay as authentic as I could. But one of our regular customers requested a scrambled egg served on a grovbirkes, and we started playing with other toppings, like bacon, cured salmon, Havarti cheese, and smoked ham. After we put this breakfast sandwich on the menu, it instantly became one of our bestselling items. A food critic from the *San Francisco Chronicle* wrote it up as one of the best things that they'd recently eaten. If you make grovbirkes, definitely save a few to treat yourself to one of these breakfast sandwiches. **MAKES 1 SANDWICH**

1 Grovbirkes (page 152), sliced in half crosswise

2 eggs

1 tablespoon unsalted butter

Kosher salt and freshly ground black pepper

1 slice Havarti cheese (about 1 ounce/ 28 g), 2 ounces (57 g) smoked ham, or 2 strips cooked bacon (or some combination of the above)

Preheat the oven to 350°F (175°C).

Toast the grovbirkes, cut side up, directly on the oven rack.

Meanwhile, in a small bowl, lightly beat the eggs with a fork or whisk.

In a small skillet, melt the butter over medium heat. Once it's melted and sizzling, add the beaten eggs. If you like a soft scramble, decrease the heat to low and stir continuously as the eggs cook. If you prefer a harder scramble, cook them at a higher temperature and stir less often. Add a pinch of salt and a few grinds of pepper. Turn off the heat when you are satisfied with the texture and doneness of your eggs.

Remove the toasted grovbirkes from the oven and place the eggs on the bottom half, followed by the cheese and/or breakfast meat, followed by the top half. There is no need to melt the cheese; the heat of the eggs will do so.

These are best eaten right away while hot, although I have been told by people who order them for delivery that they hold up for at least 1 hour, wrapped, and make a good commuter's breakfast or picnic sandwich.

SMOKED TROUT SALAD

Smoked fish is one of my all-time favorite foods, at least when it's done well. One summer, many years ago, I worked at a Danish restaurant that had a smoker in the backyard. Just before service we'd pull the hot smoked fish from the smoker, being careful while we transferred it from smoking racks to cooling trays. It was as soft as butter, literally melting on your tongue. With that fish, we'd make a smoked fish platter, and this trout salad was one of the components. Heavenly!

At Kantine, our smoked trout salad is one of the most popular items on our breakfast board, best eaten with either rye bread or rye crispbread. The recipe combines flaky smoked trout with finely minced raw celery root, which adds a lovely flavor and stretches out the relatively expensive smoked trout. Because both the smoked trout and the capers are salty, wait until the very end to add salt, only if needed. (You probably won't.) Smoked salmon also works if smoked trout is unavailable, but be sure to buy smoked fish that comes sold in thick portions (like fillets), not thin slices (like gravlax). This salad requires the flaky texture of cooked fish.

MAKES 4 TO 6 SERVINGS

5 ounces (141 g) celery root

2 tablespoons capers

½ cup (92 g) mayonnaise

½ up (92 g) crème fraîche or sour cream

1 teaspoon Dijon mustard

1 tablespoon chopped fresh dill

8 ounces (226 g) smoked trout fillets

1 to 2 teaspoons fresh lemon juice

Kosher salt and freshly ground black pepper

To finish

Sprouted Rye Bread (page 198) or Rye Crispbread (page 175) for serving

3 tablespoons pickled red onions (page 188)

¼ cup cured trout roe (optional)

Use a vegetable peeler (and a paring knife, if needed) to remove the brown skin from the celery root, then cut it into ice cube–size chunks.

In a food processor, pulse the celery root until it's the size of couscous. Transfer it to a large bowl.

Rinse the capers, squeezing out any excess water, and then finely chop them. Add them to the celery root.

In a medium bowl, whisk together the mayonnaise, crème fraîche, mustard, and dill. Add this dressing to the celery root mixture and stir to combine thoroughly.

Place the smoked trout on a baking tray or large cutting board and carefully remove the skin and bones. Smoked trout fillets contain a lot of tiny, nearly transparent bones that can be hard to spot. Comb through the fish with your fingers to get them out, as ideally no bones will sneak into your salad. Flake the deboned fish into pea-size pieces. Add the flaked fish to the celery root mixture and stir gently. Season to taste with the lemon juice, pepper, and salt, if needed.

Serve the smoked trout salad on the bread and garnish with the pickled red onions. Alternatively, you can serve the salad in small ramekins with toast or bread alongside. For an extra-special festive touch, garnish with the roe. Store the salad in an airtight container in the refrigerator for up to 3 to 4 days.

CONTINUED

PICKLED RED ONIONS

There are lots of recipes out there for pickled onions, but I like this one because it doesn't require you to boil a brine first, which makes it faster and less fussy than some other recipes. It also doesn't include any sugar, which is my preference, allowing the natural sweetness of the red onion to shine. At Kantine, we like to add a slice of raw red beet to the onions, which makes them even more vibrant in color without imparting any flavor. If you have a beet lying around, try this!

1 large red onion, halved and sliced into thin strips

1 tablespoon kosher salt

1 small slice of red beet (optional)

½ cup (116 g) red wine vinegar, plus more as needed

Place the onion in a nonreactive (glass or stainless-steel) bowl and sprinkle with the salt. Stir in the salt and let the onion sit for 15 minutes, or until limp. Add the beet (if using). Then pour enough vinegar to come halfway up the slices of onion and let that sit for about 1 hour, giving it a stir every 10 to 15 minutes.

Discard the beet slice and serve the pickled onion. Store the onion, still in the vinegar, in an airtight container in the refrigerator for up to 2 weeks.

CITRUS SALAD WITH MINT TARRAGON SUGAR

The topping on this citrus salad is inspired by a dish I had at a restaurant in Copenhagen where they pounded fresh tarragon and mint leaves into sugar that turned a bright shade of green and was sprinkled on hot porridge. Mint may seem like an obvious herb to pair with fruit, but it tastes new and exciting when combined with the sweet anise flavor of fresh tarragon. We make this mint tarragon sugar all year long at Kantine, sprinkling it on whatever fresh fruit is in season, from berries to melon to citrus. Be sure to prepare your mint tarragon sugar right before you intend to serve and eat it on fruit salad or the mint will oxidize and turn brown. It also provides a unique garnish for yogurt or porridge. MAKES 4 TO 6 SMALL SERVINGS

2 pounds (900 g) fresh citrus (see Note)

½ cup (100 g) sugar

15 to 20 fresh mint leaves

Leaves from 3 sprigs of tarragon

PREP THE CITRUS FRUIT

To prepare an orange, first cut off the top and the bottom using a sharp paring or chef's knife. Then cut a strip of the peel off from head to toe, just below the pith and following the shape of the orange. Rotate the fruit slightly clockwise so that more peel is at your knife's edge, ready to be removed. Continue cutting off the peel one strip at a time, then rotating, until the entire orange has been peeled. Next, remove and discard the core. Divide the oranges between the bowls in which you plan to serve the salad. Do the same for bigger citrus fruits like grapefruits and pomelos, then cut the segments into about 1-inch (2.5 cm) chunks, adding them to the bowls with the oranges.

WHEN READY TO SERVE, MAKE THE MINT TARRAGON SUGAR

You can use a spice grinder if that's all you have, but I think it's better to do this by hand in a mortar and pestle because you will have more control. Place the sugar, mint, and tarragon in a mortar. Begin by making a circular rotation, grinding the leaves against the sides of the mortar. Then alternate between pounding and rotating. As you go, the leaves will become completely pulverized and eventually turn the sugar a lovely shade of green. In the end, remove any stems you may find.

Sprinkle some of the mint tarragon sugar over your citrus fruit and serve right away.

NOTE I recommend a mixture of blood oranges, Cara Cara oranges, pomelo, and grapefruit, or whatever citrus look the best and are in season.

RYE BREAD PORRIDGE

Øllebrød

Making porridge out of rye bread is a great way to transform the crusty leftovers of home-baked bread into something warm and comforting. In the olden days, Danes used to soak stale bread in a malty and sweet white beer. When I first moved to Denmark, the notion of eating a porridge made from old bread and beer didn't appeal to me. But I gave it a try and was pleasantly surprised. In my take on this porridge, beer is replaced with water, citrus juice and zest add zing, and mashed banana and honey give it sweetness. To make this part of a special breakfast spread, serve it with sweetened whipped cream, apple compote (see page 155) or roasted fruit, and toasted coconut. I recommend ladling it into shallow bowls, as this gives the porridge a chance to cool down and maximizes the topping-to-porridge ratio. Each spoonful should hold half porridge and half whipped cream and other toppings. MAKES 4 TO 6 SERVINGS

3½ cups (400 g) 1-inch (2.5 cm) pieces torn rye bread (stale is good)

4 cups (1 liter) water

1 ripe, soft banana

2 tablespoons honey

Zest and juice of 1 orange

½ teaspoon ground cinnamon

¼ teaspoon freshly ground decorticated cardamom (see page 21)

¼ teaspoon ground cloves

To finish

1 cup (70 g) unsweetened flaked or shredded coconut

1 cup (226 g) heavy cream

3 tablespoons powdered sugar

Cardamom sugar (see page 77)

Fruit compote, chunks of orange, grated pear, or diced apple (optional)

Place the pieces of bread in a large heavy-bottomed saucepan. Add the water and then let the bread sit, soaking in the water, until it has softened and puffed up, at least 15 minutes.

When you are ready to cook the porridge, preheat the oven to 350°F (175°C).

Use a whisk or wooden spoon to break up the soaked bread. Place the saucepan on the stove and bring to a simmer over medium heat. Add the banana and mash it into the mixture. Add the honey, orange zest and juice, cinnamon, cardamom, and cloves and stir. Simmer the mixture for about 10 minutes, stirring occasionally so that it doesn't stick to the bottom of the pan. You want some of the moisture to cook off so that your porridge achieves a consistency between a thin oatmeal and a thick potato soup.

While the porridge is cooking, sprinkle the coconut onto an unlined baking tray and toast in the oven for 10 minutes, stirring halfway through so that it gets evenly browned.

In the bowl of a stand mixer fitted with the whisk attachment or in a large bowl with a handheld mixer, whip the cream on medium until soft peaks form (see page 37). Add the powdered sugar and whip again.

Serve the porridge in shallow bowls, topped with mounds of the soft whipped cream and sprinkled with the toasted coconut and cardamom sugar. Top with fruit compote or fresh fruit like chunks of orange, grated pear, or diced apple. I recommend serving this family-style, with bowls of toppings to be passed around. That way the whipped cream stays fluffy throughout the meal. This porridge is best when every bite includes toppings. Rye porridge can be made ahead, cooled, and stored in an airtight container in the refrigerator for up to 5 days. Reheat thoroughly on the stovetop and serve as above.

RUNNY EGG WITH SPINACH CREAM

This was one of the first recipes that we offered with the brunch board at Kantine, where I was seeking a simple egg dish that would provide warm morning comfort to our guests. For each serving, a puree of cooked spinach and cream gets ladled into a small bowl. A perfectly soft-boiled egg rests in this bright green sauce, which melds with the runny yolk as it's pierced by a spoon. Whereas an American breakfast often puts eggs at the center of the meal, this is an egg side dish to be enjoyed as part of a larger Scandinavian spread along with Sprouted Rye Bread (page 198) or Soft Flatbread (page 173), Havarti cheese, Smoked Trout Salad (page 187), and/or Citrus Salad with Mint Tarragon Sugar (page 189). MAKES 4 TO 6 SERVINGS

4 to 6 eggs (1 egg per person)

2 teaspoons olive oil

8 ounces (226 g) baby spinach, washed

1¼ cups (300 g) heavy cream

½ teaspoon kosher salt, plus more as needed

To finish

Freshly ground black pepper

A few sprigs of fresh herbs (dill, tarragon, or another fresh herb that you like)

MAKE THE SOFT-BOILED EGGS

Bring a medium pot of water to a boil over high heat. Carefully lower the eggs into the boiling water and set a timer for 6½ minutes. While the eggs are boiling, prepare a large bowl of ice and water in the sink. As soon as your timer goes off, transfer the eggs to the ice bath. This is called "shocking" the eggs, which means abruptly stopping the cooking process. Otherwise, they will continue to cook in their hot shells even after you remove them from the boiling water. Allow them to soak in the ice bath until they feel cold to the touch.

Gently peel each egg. To do this, I like to crack the top of the egg and use a teaspoon to gently get under the membrane and loosen up the shell (see photographs on page 192). Once your eggs are all peeled, set them aside while you make the spinach cream, or store them in an airtight container in the refrigerator for up to 2 days.

In a large skillet over medium-high heat, heat the olive oil until a bead of water sizzles in the pan. Add the baby spinach by the handful, stirring as it wilts and continuing to add more until it is all in the pan. Continue to cook the spinach for 2 to 3 minutes and don't add any salt yet. It's easy to oversalt spinach as it looks like so much but then reduces to comparatively little by the end, so I recommend salting once the spinach is fully cooked. Transfer the spinach to a bowl for about 5 minutes, until it's cool enough to handle.

While the spinach is cooling, bring a medium pot of water to a boil over high heat.

Wring out any extra liquid from the spinach over the sink and then place it in a blender, along with ¾ cup (180 g) of the cream and the salt. Pulse to blend. You want to do this as quickly as you can so that you don't risk the cream turning to butter. Transfer the puree to a small saucepan over low heat and stir in the remaining ½ cup (120 g) of cream as the mixture reheats. Season with more salt, if needed, and the pepper. The puree should have a uniform green color and creamy texture.

Right before serving, turn the heat off below the pot containing the boiled water and place the peeled soft-boiled eggs in the pot for exactly 2 minutes, just to heat them through.

Distribute the spinach sauce among individual serving bowls and place an egg in each one. Sprinkle each with a little salt, garnish with a leaf or two of the fresh herbs, and serve right away on your Scandinavian brunch table.

RYE BREAD AND SMØRREBRØD

Rye bread is to Denmark what baguettes are to France. Danish rugbrød, or rye bread, is springy, substantial, and filling. It holds its shape when thinly sliced, which is a must for Danish smørrebrød, the open-faced sandwiches that many Danes eat for lunch. I fell in love with Danish rye bread at a cute little bakery called Bageriet Brød, around the corner from our first apartment in Copenhagen. *Brød* means "bread," and it was a word I struggled to pronounce while learning Danish. I used to practice for my new friends behind the counter while buying pastries and bread to take home.

For most people in Denmark, rye bread is something they buy at the bakery or grocery store, not something they commonly bake from scratch. I'd made it a few times over the years in a professional capacity but was not an expert in any way by the time we left Denmark seven years ago and came to California. So, when we settled into life in San Francisco and I made up my mind to bake and start selling the Danish rye that our family and other Scandinavian expats were missing, I had to create a recipe that would work with American ingredients, particularly flour, which differs from the flours I baked with in Denmark.

I started developing my recipe in the not particularly well-equipped kitchen of our first rental house, making little tweaks with each loaf until I was convinced that I had the recipe right. My rye bread is not made entirely of rye flour, as that would produce a denser loaf than I was going for. I add sprouted rye berries (see page 25), as I love the texture they bring to the loaf. While it takes a couple of days for the berries to sprout, it's simple to do and would be a fun project to undertake with a child, as you watch a tiny thread of growth push its way out of the tip of each soaked rye berry.

Speaking of kids, I was lucky to have my teenage daughter Rosa's help selling my loaves of bread and open-faced sandwiches at the Ferry Building farmers' market, which was my first culinary venture in California. Rosa worked the register while I served customers, chatting and getting to know those who returned each week. Their appreciation and sustained business gave me the courage to open a Scandinavian restaurant with a more extensive menu.

I still sell lots of freshly baked loaves of rye bread at Kantine and serve it as the base of smørrebrød and as an accompaniment to many dishes. It's as good untoasted as it is toasted and terrific used in a grilled cheese sandwich or dunked in hot soup. It's a versatile, hearty, and nourishing seeded loaf of bread that I think you'll agree tastes different from others out there already.

SPROUTED RYE BREAD

Rugbrød

This is the bread that I first sold at the San Francisco Ferry Building farmers' market. Once we put out a basket of small chunks of sample bread, people started coming to our stand week after week. This recipe requires you to first sprout rye berries, which are the whole-grain form of rye flour with only the hull removed (see page 25). These berries are available online and can be purchased in bulk at some health food stores and shops featuring organic ingredients. When using rye berries in this recipe, begin by soaking them in water for several hours and then placing the soaked berries on a baking tray, covered, for an additional day. While this process is simple and straightforward, do make sure to allot the time you need for the sprouting to happen, about two days before you want to bake your bread.

At Kantine, we use a natural leavener (like a sourdough starter). Our previous leavener was nicknamed Barack Doughbama before its name changed to Marilyn Mondough. This starter allows us to bake rye bread without commercial yeast. But for the novice home baker, dry yeast makes producing a good loaf a lot easier. However, I encourage you to set aside a half cup of the dough each time you make this bread, storing it in the refrigerator in an airtight container, to add to future loaves. This will give your bread some of the delicious natural tanginess of a sourdough leavener.

If you have two loaf pans, definitely consider doubling this recipe. That way you'll have enough bread for sandwiches, plus more for making Rye Bread Porridge (page 190) and Rye and Oat Granola (page 183). **MAKES ONE 9 BY 5-INCH (23 BY 13 CM) LOAF**

- ¼ cup plus 2 tablespoons (60 g) rye berries
- 1 cup (240 g) hot water
- ⅔ cup (150 g) buttermilk
- 1½ teaspoons active dry yeast
- 1 tablespoon malt syrup (see page 24)
- 1 cup (128 g) all-purpose flour
- 1¼ cups (150 g) rye flour
- Vegetable oil for greasing

Two to 4 days before you want to bake the bread, begin by sprouting your rye berries. This makes them softer and sweeter, adding a nice flavor and chewy texture. Soak the rye berries in a bowl of room-temperature water, covered by about 1 inch (2.5 cm), for a minimum of 6 hours and up to 12 hours. Thoroughly drain the soaked rye berries in a fine-mesh strainer and spread them out on the bottom of a loaf pan. Cover the pan with a clean kitchen towel and keep it out at room temperature until they begin to sprout. This will take about 1 day, possibly longer if the air is cold. If the air is very warm, you may need to occasionally sprinkle them with water and move them around with your fingers so that they don't dry out completely. Look for a tiny filament sprouting from one end of the rye berry. You may notice them moving a little, if you look very closely, as they sprout before your very eyes! Don't let the sprouts grow too long or the rye berries may taste too sweet. Once a little thread has emerged from most of the berries, transfer the sprouts to an airtight container and store them in the refrigerator, where they will keep for up to 2 days.

On baking day, in the bowl of a stand mixer, stir together the hot water and buttermilk. Use a digital thermometer to measure the temperature:

105° to 110°F (40° to 43°C) is the ideal temperature for the yeast to bloom. Add the yeast and malt syrup, whisking to combine, and let the mixture sit for 10 minutes. Then add the all-purpose and rye flours. Using the paddle attachment, mix on medium speed until well blended. Let this mixture rest for 30 minutes.

While the dough is resting, lightly oil a 9 by 5-inch (23 by 13 cm) loaf pan and line it with parchment paper. Cut it to fit the pan lengthwise, with flaps of 1 to 2 inches (2.5 to 5 cm), hanging over the two longer sides of the pan, so that you can lift the baked loaf out.

When the dough is done resting, add the salt, sunflower seeds, flax seeds, pumpkin seeds, sesame seeds, and sprouted rye berries and mix with the paddle attachment on medium until well combined.

Scoop out ¼ cup (50 g) of the dough. Place it in an airtight container, and refrigerate for up to 3 weeks, so that it will ferment and you can add it to your dough the next time you bake this bread, lending it a pleasant depth of flavor. Keep doing this every time you bake rye bread, always reserving ¼ cup (50 g) for your next loaf.

Transfer the remaining dough to the prepared loaf pan. It should fill the pan about three-quarters of the way to the top. Cover the pan with a clean kitchen towel or plastic wrap, being careful to stretch it tight so that it doesn't come into contact with the dough, and let it proof for about 1 hour. The rise time can vary slightly depending on the temperature of your kitchen. You'll know it's ready when the dough appears fluffy and there are tiny air bubbles bursting on the surface.

About 30 minutes into the proofing, preheat the oven to 500°F (260°C).

Put the loaf in the oven and immediately throw a cup of water onto the bottom of the oven to create steam. Close the oven door and decrease the temperature to 275°F (135°C).

Bake for 1 hour, then use a digital thermometer to check the temperature at the center of the loaf. It should read 210°F (100°C). If it's lower, return the bread to the oven and keep checking every 5 minutes until the center of the loaf reaches this temperature.

After taking the pan from the oven, immediately remove the bread by tipping the pan onto its side, tugging on the parchment paper, and tapping the bread out. Let it cool overnight for the best slicing, although I won't blame you if you can't resist lopping off the hot heel and smearing it with a thick layer of cold butter. Store the cooled bread wrapped in parchment paper or a clean kitchen towel at room temperature, where it will stay fresh for up to 3 days, or in the refrigerator for up to 1 week.

1½ teaspoons kosher salt

⅓ cup (40 g) sunflower seeds

⅓ cup (50 g) flax seeds

5 tablespoons (25 g) pumpkin seeds

5 tablespoons (25 g) sesame seeds

HOW TO MAKE AND EAT SMØRREBRØD: A MASTER CLASS IN LAYERING

It is no exaggeration to say that smørrebrød, or open-faced sandwiches, are the classic Danish dish. While an open-faced sandwich might not seem all that exciting to the uninitiated, Danes have made it an art form. In the nineteenth century, the onset of industrialization meant that factory workers couldn't return home for lunch, and they needed something portable and hearty that could last until midday. Butter (or goose fat) spread on rye bread ensured that whatever meat or fish (usually left over from dinner the night before) got heaped on top wouldn't seep through and make the bread soggy.

Some aspects of the original remain to this day. *Smørrebrød* literally means "butter bread," and butter is still smeared on a slice of bread from crust to crust before other toppings get added. Nowadays, in addition to fish, cold cuts, and sliced cheese, various spreads and garnishes, such as potato salad, hummus, microgreens, veggie chips, and other contemporary toppings, might find their way onto a beautiful smørrebrød. Entire restaurants are devoted to these open-faced sandwiches, where extraordinary care is given to layering the components on smørrebrød in a way that is as visually pleasing as it is delicious.

Smørrebrød are served across all strata of society, from extremely fancy restaurants to working-class lunch counters, where they often come accompanied by a fist-size meatball or a fried fish cake. You can experiment and take some liberties in creating your own open-faced sandwiches. For instance, if you have a fantastic ripe avocado, go ahead and slice it to add on top, even though that is not a traditional Scandinavian garnish. However, there are some rules to be followed if you want this to count as an authentic smørrebrød experience rather than a plate of avocado toast.

Follow these rules as they add to your enjoyment, always keeping the visual element in mind as you create your sandwich. With fresh rye bread, good-quality butter, and whatever toppings you choose, your smørrebrød are bound to be works of delectable art. The recipes in this chapter are some of my favorite smørrebrød combinations. Feel free to make them as is or get creative and listen to your own sandwich muse!

HERE ARE TEN RULES FOR MAKING AND EATING SMØRREBRØD THAT I LEARNED ON THE GROUND:

1 Choose attractive slices of bread to serve as your blank "canvas" (never the heel).

2 Make your smørrebrød on a small and handy cutting board from which you can easily transfer it to a plate. Otherwise, it's hard to lift the finished sandwich without having it collapse, and it keeps the edges of your plate clean.

3 Always begin by buttering the whole slice of bread from crust to crust, going to the edge but never over the edge. The rare exception to the butter rule might be if you wanted a layer of hummus on your bread instead. But even then, many Danes would apply butter beneath the hummus.

4 Don't heap on toppings, but distribute them evenly from crust to crust, doing so in a visually pleasing manner (for instance, arranging slices of hard-boiled egg in a shingled pattern or overlapping smoked salmon so as to hide the darker bottom of each slice). Again, go to but never over the edge.

5 Any cooked components (like eggs, shrimp, or vegetables) should be prepared as lightly as possible to keep everything tasting fresh and bright.

6 Shrimp and salmon are often served on white rather than rye bread, but I personally prefer rye for all smørrebrød and break this rule without apology.

7 Add mayonnaise, aioli, or rémoulade in a dollop on top of fresh ingredients, if desired. At smørrebrød restaurant kitchens in Denmark, this is often done with a squeeze bottle to keep things looking neat.

8 When serving or ordering a meal of smørrebrød, people typically begin with herring, then move on to fish and shrimp before concluding the meal with meat and cheese.

9 Smørrebrød should please the eye as much as the palate and also include a variety of flavors (like bitter and sweet) as well as textures (like crispy and creamy). Use sprigs of fresh herbs to garnish at the end. Dill fronds are always pretty, as well as torn leaves of flat-leaf parsley or sliced chives. If you happen to have edible flowers in your garden, don't be afraid to garnish with them! My favorites include marigold, tulip, nasturtium, violets, English daisies, calendula, dandelion, and even carnation! To garnish in a Scandinavian manner, use only the petals, not the whole flower.

10 Smørrebrød is not to be picked up and eaten with your hands but rather left on a plate and enjoyed with a knife and fork. You'll soon understand why after you make one, since lifting one of these to your mouth would result in a messy lap.

SWEET POTATO, GOAT CHEESE, AND APPLE SMØRREBRØD

Traditional Danish open-faced sandwiches are topped with meat or fish and skimp on the vegetables. Modern smørrebrød, however, break that old framework, and you can now find splendid plant-forward options in Denmark. Our talented line cook Charlie Richardson concocted the idea behind this sandwich, and as soon as we tasted it, we knew it was a winner. The combination of soft sweet potatoes; salty, tangy goat cheese; crunchy, toasted walnuts; and crisp and tart apples brings a range of textures and tastes to each bite. Goat cheese is a favorite ingredient of mine, but a crumbly blue or feta would work just as well. While roasting the sweet potatoes takes an hour (be sure to factor that into your prep time), this smørrebrød is quick to assemble. MAKES 6 SANDWICHES

2 pounds (900 g) sweet potato

½ cup (60 g) walnuts

1 tablespoon olive oil

1 clove garlic, minced

⅓ cup (75 g) sour cream

1 teaspoon kosher salt, plus more as needed

¼ teaspoon freshly ground decorticated cardamom (see page 21)

2 large green apples (such as Granny Smith or similar)

For assembly

6 freshly cut slices Sprouted Rye Bread (page 198)

1 tablespoon unsalted butter, at room temperature

½ cup (75 g) goat cheese

Freshly ground black pepper

2 to 3 tablespoons minced fresh herbs

Preheat the oven to 375°F (190°C).

Place the sweet potatoes on a baking tray and bake for about 1 hour, until deflated and very soft. Let the sweet potatoes cool before handling.

Meanwhile, place the walnuts on a separate baking tray and toast them in the oven until lightly browned, 6 to 8 minutes. Let the walnuts cool, then coarsely chop them.

Remove and discard the sweet potato skins and transfer the flesh to a medium bowl and, using a fork or whisk, mash the sweet potatoes into a semismooth puree with only small chunks remaining.

In a small saucepan over low heat, heat the olive oil and garlic until it just begins to sizzle, without browning. Add the garlic oil to the sweet potatoes. Stir in the sour cream, salt, and cardamom.

Cut the four sides off each apple, discarding the core. Thinly slice each apple chunk. It is important to slice the apple shortly before assembling the smørrebrød so that it doesn't turn brown.

ASSEMBLE

Lay the bread slices on a work surface. Lightly butter each slice all the way to the edges but not over. Divide the sweet potato mixture among the slices, spreading it in an even layer, again being mindful to spread to the edges of the bread but not over. Arrange the apple slices over top (use about one-quarter of an apple per sandwich) in one direction, with the green skin upward and shingled across. Using two small spoons, drop four or five pea-size pieces of the goat cheese over each sandwich. Sprinkle each with the walnuts and a pinch of salt and grind of pepper, and garnish with the fresh herbs. Serve immediately.

ROASTED CAULIFLOWER, TARRAGON CREAM, AND ALMOND SMØRREBRØD

When I first moved to the Bay Area, I was struck by the bounty, variety, and quality of local produce available at farmers' markets. A chef's dream come true! This vegetarian sandwich was originally created as an ode to cauliflower and romanesco, and I encourage you to use both if you have access. For those who don't, it's delicious made solely with cauliflower. Oven-roasted cauliflower on its own is underrated, and it's even better when paired with good bread and a cold herb sauce. It isn't ideal to reheat roasted cauliflower, so I suggest that you roast the cauliflower on the day that you want to eat these sandwiches, letting it cool to room temperature and never refrigerating it. MAKES 6 SANDWICHES

1 head cauliflower and 1 head romanesco (or 2 heads cauliflower; about 2½ pounds/1.1 kg total)

½ teaspoon kosher salt

3 tablespoons extra-virgin olive oil

¼ cup (40 g) almond slivers

Tarragon cream

Leaves from 2 bunches of tarragon, chopped (about ¼ cup), plus more for garnish

5 tablespoons (76 g) sour cream

2 tablespoons mayonnaise

2 teaspoons fresh lemon juice

1 teaspoon Dijon mustard

Kosher salt and freshly ground black pepper

For assembly

6 freshly cut slices Sprouted Rye Bread (page 198)

1 tablespoon unsalted butter, at room temperature

Preheat the oven to 375°F (175°C).

Cut the cauliflower and romanesco (if using) in half, remove and discard the stems, and break the florets into 1½- to 2-inch (3.5 to 5 cm) pieces. In a medium bowl, toss the florets together with the salt and olive oil until lightly coated. Spread the florets out on two baking trays, being sure to leave space between the florets as this allows air to crisp their tips, and bake for 35 to 45 minutes, until golden brown and tender.

Place the almonds in an oven-safe dish and toast them in the oven with the cauliflower for the last 15 minutes of its roasting time, until golden brown. Let both the cauliflower and almonds cool to room temperature.

MEANWHILE, MAKE THE TARRAGON CREAM

In a small bowl, mix together the tarragon, sour cream, mayonnaise, lemon juice, and mustard. Season to taste with salt and pepper. You should be able to taste the tarragon as well as the zing from the lemon juice and mustard. Cover and refrigerate until ready to serve.

ASSEMBLE

Lay the bread slices on a work surface. Lightly butter each slice, making sure to butter all the way to the edges but not over. Top each slice of bread with about 1 tablespoon of the tarragon cream and spread it out completely. (Any extra sauce makes an excellent condiment for grilled fish or meat!) Arrange the cauliflower carefully over the top, covering the entire surface of each slice with the most appealing bits and pieces facing up. Give the smørrebrød a sprinkle of salt and a grind of pepper and garnish each with a large pinch of the almonds and a sprinkle of tarragon. Serve immediately.

EGG AND SHRIMP SMØRREBRØD

I think of myself as an "egg girl." The term was coined by my Danish friend Caroline Gjerulff, with whom I have had many good conversations while eating a 4-minute egg. Like me, she loves eating eggs in all variations under the sun, and this is her favorite smørrebrød, featuring a combination of hard-boiled eggs and cooked shrimp. Some Danes believe that because shrimp have such a delicate flavor, it's nicer to serve them on white bread, where they won't compete with the seeds or malt in rye, but because this is just as much an egg sandwich as a shrimp sandwich, I prefer it on rye. As with all smørrebrød, assemble this open-faced sandwich on a small cutting board so that it's easy to pick up and transfer to a plate without precious shrimp tumbling off. MAKES 6 SANDWICHES

6 freshly cut slices Sprouted Rye Bread (page 198)

2 tablespoons unsalted butter, at room temperature

8 hard-boiled eggs (see page 208), peeled and sliced into disks

3 cups (300 g) cooked bay shrimp (small pink shrimp, which can be bought frozen and thawed)

1 teaspoon fresh lemon juice

½ teaspoon kosher salt

3 tablespoons finely sliced fresh chives

2 tablespoons mayonnaise

5 or 6 sprigs of dill

Lay the bread slices on a work surface. Lightly butter each slice, being sure to butter all the way to the edges but not over. Arrange the slices of hard-boiled egg in a shingled pattern covering the bread. You'll want to use at least 1 egg per slice of bread. Place the end slices of egg (without the yolk) in the middle, where they will get hidden beneath the shrimp. Place about ⅔ cup (115 g) of the shrimp at the center of each slice of bread, nicely mounded over the shingled hard-boiled eggs. Drizzle the lemon juice and sprinkle the salt across each mound of shrimp, then scatter them with the chives. Add about 1 teaspoon of the mayonnaise on top of each sandwich. In restaurant kitchens in Denmark, condiments like this are often applied using a squeeze bottle, which makes a perfectly shaped bead, but it's tricky to fill a squeeze bottle with mayonnaise so I recommend just using a spoon but doing so carefully. As a final touch, lay a few sprigs of the dill on top of each sandwich as a pretty garnish. Serve immediately.

PERFECT HARD-BOILED EGGS

While a hard-boiled egg epitomizes simplicity, simple doesn't always mean easy. As if to prove it, there are an astonishing number of different ways that people suggest hard- or soft-boiling an egg, from cooking them in an Instant Pot to bringing water to a boil, then turning the stove off to let them finish cooking as the water cools. I don't like having to use a lot of equipment for such an elemental task, and I prefer being able to control the cooking process to achieve the perfect yolk. Overcooked hard-boiled egg yolks get that unappealing green tinge, which is especially displeasing when you're going to be slicing them to arrange on a pretty Danish sandwich. My favorite method is actually quite simple and lets you control the results, so your yolks come out just as you like them. If you want to be extra sure that they look nice, I recommend boiling them on the day that you are going to serve them, as refrigerator storage can also lead to that green tinge. Older eggs (about 1 week) will be easier to peel after they are boiled.

Place eggs in a pot and cover with cold water by 1 inch (2.5 cm). Bring to a boil over high heat. As soon as it comes to a full boil, lower the heat to medium-high and immediately set a timer. For firm yolks, boil the eggs for 8 minutes. For creamier yolks, 6 to 7 minutes. Soft-boiled eggs need only 4 minutes. While the eggs cook, create an ice-water bath by filling a large bowl with water and ample ice cubes. As soon as your timer goes off, use a slotted spoon to remove the eggs from the boiling water and transfer them to the ice bath. Don't skip this step as the ice makes their shells and sticky membrane easy to peel off. Let them soak until they are cool to the touch, then peel to use or store in their shells in the refrigerator.

CHICKEN SALAD WITH OYSTER MUSHROOMS AND SORREL SMØRREBRØD

Chicken salad is one of my favorite things to serve and to eat for lunch. Chicken salad made from scratch seems impressive, but it's barely more difficult than making tuna salad, especially if you happen to have leftover chicken. If that's not the case, have no fear: I'm providing directions for cooking chicken from scratch to cover all bases. This chicken salad derives its uniquely tart taste from sorrel, an herb that grows wild in many parts of the world. In Ohio as a kid, whenever my sister and I went on hikes, we loved to munch on sour grass, also known as wood sorrel. Varieties of the herb grow in California and Denmark, too. The kind that grows here in San Francisco has heart-shaped leaves and tiny yellow flowers. If you don't find sorrel at your favorite grocer, then it's time to go foraging like a Scandinavian! And if your hunt ends fruitless, I'd use fresh tarragon and dill instead of omitting. It's the freshness from the herbs that make this chicken salad so extraordinary. Actually no, it's the fact that you're making chicken salad from scratch. Kudos to you and enjoy! **MAKES 6 SANDWICHES**

Chicken salad

3 tablespoons extra-virgin olive oil

2½ pounds (1.1 kg) bone-in, skin-on chicken thighs (for about 2½ cups /350 g cooked)

1 teaspoon kosher salt

Freshly ground black pepper

12 ounces (340 g) oyster mushrooms (about 1 cup cooked)

¾ cup (90 g) diced celery (reserve any leaves for garnish)

2 tablespoons minced shallot

½ cup (160 g) mayonnaise

¾ cup (192 g) sour cream

Finely grated zest of 1 lemon

→ INGREDIENTS CONTINUED

MAKE THE SALAD

Line a 13 by 18-inch (33 by 46 cm) baking tray with parchment paper. Preheat the oven to 375°F (175°C).

In a large bowl, pour 1 tablespoon of the olive oil over the chicken thighs and season with the salt and pepper. Place the thighs, skin side up, on the prepared baking tray.

Bake the chicken thighs for 30 to 40 minutes, or until they reach an internal temperature of 165°F (75°C). The timing will depend greatly on the size of the thighs, so start checking after 30 minutes and then at 5-minute intervals after that. Allow the chicken to cool to room temperature.

Meanwhile, prepare the oyster mushrooms. Pull the mushroom clusters apart and tear the larger mushrooms in half, so that they are all roughly the same size.

In a large skillet, heat the remaining 2 tablespoons olive oil over medium-high heat. Add the mushrooms and wait 3 to 4 minutes before giving them a stir, so they can sear and brown. Continue to cook, stirring occasionally, until the mushrooms have gone limp and are golden in color, 7 to 8 minutes. Transfer the mushrooms to a plate and allow them to cool.

CONTINUED

CHICKEN SALAD WITH OYSTER MUSHROOMS AND SORREL SMØRREBRØD, CONTINUED

1 tablespoon fresh lemon juice

1 tablespoon Dijon mustard

3 tablespoons chopped fresh sorrel

For assembly

6 freshly cut slices Sprouted Rye Bread (page 198)

2 tablespoons unsalted butter, at room temperature

Garnish (optional)

6 to 8 slices cooked bacon

Small bowl of Dijon mustard

Remove and discard the chicken thigh bones and cartilage and dice the meat. In a large bowl, combine the chicken, mushrooms, celery, shallot, mayonnaise, sour cream, lemon zest and juice, mustard, and 2 tablespoons of the sorrel. Stir everything to combine and adjust the seasonings, if needed. If not serving immediately, store the chicken salad in an airtight container in the refrigerator for up to 3 days.

ASSEMBLE

Lay the bread slices on a work surface. Lightly butter each slice, being sure to butter all the way to the edges but not over. Divide the chicken salad among the bread slices. Arrange the salad in an even layer on the surface of the bread, making sure to bring the salad all the way to the edges but not over. Garnish each sandwich with some of the remaining 1 tablespoon sorrel and the reserved celery leaves and serve immediately. As an optional garnish, serve the sandwiches with a side of crispy bacon and a little dish of Dijon mustard, so that those who wish to do so may crumble the bacon onto their sandwiches.

RUSSIAN HERRING SALAD WITH BEETS AND APPLE SMØRREBRØD

At any Scandinavian supermarket, you're bound to find a refrigerated wall of jars of pickled herring. They always have basic herring in white wine marinade, as well as other preparations where the fish has been combined with a creamy sauce flavored with ingredients like whole-grain mustard, curry spices, or sour cream and herbs. I immediately took to pickled herring and found fish marinated in creamy dressings to be especially tasty. American supermarkets don't typically carry anything other than marinated herring, so I make my own creamy homemade sauce and mix it with the herring I'm able to find. MAKES 6 SANDWICHES

Russian herring salad

- 2 medium red beets, unpeeled
- 1 teaspoon kosher salt, plus more if needed
- 12 ounces (340 g) white wine–marinated herring fillet, drained well and cut into ½-inch (1 cm) pieces
- 1 crisp Granny Smith or other tart and crunchy apple, peeled, cored, and diced into ½-inch (1 cm) cubes
- ½ cup (90 g) dill pickle slices, drained and minced
- 1 small red onion, minced
- 2 tablespoons capers, rinsed, drained, and minced
- ¾ cup (192 g) sour cream
- ¼ cup (80 g) mayonnaise
- 2 ounces (56 g) fresh horseradish, peeled
- Freshly ground black pepper

For assembly

- 6 freshly cut slices Sprouted Rye Bread (page 198)
- 1 tablespoon unsalted butter, at room temperature
- 6 soft-boiled eggs (see page 191), peeled and cut in half (optional)
- A few sprigs of parsley or other fresh herb

MAKE THE SALAD

Place the beets in a medium pot and add cold water to cover by about 1 inch (2.5 cm). Add the salt and bring to a boil over high heat. Decrease the temperature to low and simmer the beets for 20 to 40 minutes, depending on how big they are. As they finish cooking, you will see their skins slipping off. Test for doneness with a fork. Cooked beets should have the consistency of boiled potatoes. Drain them in a colander and rinse under cold water, removing any remaining skin. Pat them dry. With a chef's knife, dice the beets into ½-inch (1 cm) cubes.

In a medium bowl, stir together the beets, herring, apple, pickles, onion, capers, sour cream, and mayonnaise until it forms a creamy salad. Using a Microplane, grate in 1 tablespoon of the horseradish and stir to combine. Season to taste with salt and pepper. You may not need to add much salt at all since the herring will already be salty. Cover the herring salad and refrigerate until ready to serve.

ASSEMBLE

Lay the bread slices on a work surface. Lightly butter each side all the way to the edges of each slice but not over. Distribute the salad among the slices and spread it evenly. If desired, top each sandwich with 1 soft-boiled egg, cut in half, yolk side up. Grate the remaining horseradish directly onto each smørrebrød. Garnish with a few torn leaves of parsley or other fresh herb. Serve immediately.

GRAVLAX AND CHIVE POTATO SALAD SMØRREBRØD

Just about nothing beats the combination of silky cured salmon and creamy potato salad. This smørrebrød is one that my daughter Rosa and I made and sold together at our Ferry Building farmers' market stall, and it remains Rosa's favorite. In the United States, potato salad is often left quite chunky, but this one gets mashed to a smooth consistency that forms a pleasing contrast to crunchy sliced fennel and radishes. If you want to shave your fennel or radishes ahead of time, store them submerged in water in an airtight container in the refrigerator so that they don't discolor. **MAKES 6 SANDWICHES**

Chive potato salad

¾ pound (340 g) large potatoes

½ teaspoon kosher salt, plus more as needed

1½ cups (288 g) sour cream

1 bunch of chives, thinly sliced

2 teaspoons fresh lemon juice

For assembly

6 freshly cut slices Sprouted Rye Bread (page 198)

2 tablespoons unsalted butter, at room temperature

10 to 12 ounces (285 to 340 g) gravlax, thinly sliced (preferably wild and unsmoked)

1 fennel bulb, shaved on a mandoline or finely sliced, plus the fronds

3 radishes, shaved on a mandoline or finely sliced

1 teaspoon extra-virgin olive oil

1 teaspoon fresh lemon juice

Pinch of kosher salt

MAKE THE SALAD

Place the potatoes in a medium pot and add cold water to cover by 1 inch (2.5 cm). Add salt, and bring to a boil over high heat. Cook the potatoes until fork-tender, 20 to 30 minutes, depending on their size. Drain the potatoes, then, when they are cool enough to handle, peel each potato with a paring knife—the skin should come off easily. Transfer the potato flesh to a medium bowl. Using a ricer or potato masher, puree the potatoes. This potato salad should be as creamy as you can get it, so if you are using using a masher, keep on mashing until no lumps remain. Stir in the sour cream, half of the chives, the lemon juice, and the salt. Taste and add more salt, if needed. Cover the potato salad and refrigerate until ready to serve.

ASSEMBLE

Lay the bread slices on a work surface. Lightly butter each slice, being sure to butter all the way to the edges but not over. Spread ¼ cup (50 g) of the chive potato salad on each slice of bread, being careful that it goes to the edges but not over. Shingle the gravlax from the top down, placing the darker edge of the fish on the bottom and arranging each subsequent slice so that it covers the dark section that was closest to the fish skin. Make sure to place the slices all the way to the edges of the bread but not over. Divide the fennel and radishes among the sandwiches and top with a drizzle each of olive oil and lemon juice, plus a pinch of salt. Garnish each sandwich with fennel fronds and the remaining chives and serve immediately.

WINTER THERAPY

While the first summer I spent as an eighteen-year-old in Copenhagen was blissful, I left long before the days grew dark and short. My first winter in Denmark after returning as a grown and newly married woman was pretty rough. I couldn't yet speak the language, I didn't know a lot of people, and the relentless darkness and bitter cold got to me. While I knew that Danes loved those bright summer nights because they came as a relief after a long and equally dark winter, experiencing it on the (icy) ground was different.

At first, I mostly stayed indoors where it was warm, wondering how I was going to get through it. But then I noticed that Danes didn't seem to mind the winter at all. Unlike me, they kept right on biking down the snowplowed bike lanes of Copenhagen. To my amazement, when I did venture out, I saw people down by the harbor stripping off their clothes and jumping into the slushy water. Rather than hating the winter, they actually seemed to love it! Vinterterapi, or "winter therapy," means that people believe they derive therapeutic benefits from winter-specific activities. It's the opposite of sitting in front of a bright light to try and boost your mood. It's all about the surprising joy of embracing this season of cold and darkness, getting out and taking pleasure in winter.

I decided to follow the Danish way and lean into winter. I signed up for Danish lessons and rode my own bike through the snow to get to my classes. And I spent many happy hours hanging out with my wonderful new mother-in-law, who wasn't much of a cook but made up for it as a baker. She graciously offered to teach me how to bake her favorite Scandinavian holiday cookies. My fondest memories of that first winter are set in her kitchen, helping to bake tray after tray of cookies with which to fill her tin. She always had homemade treats to offer visitors who popped by: cookies or freshly baked cake redolent with warming spices like cinnamon, ginger, and, of course, cardamom.

As my Danish improved and the holidays neared, I was invited to julehygge at new friends' homes. This translates to the special coziness of holiday gatherings. We usually enjoyed Æbleskiver (page 236), round dumplings cooked in a special pan that are eaten after being dipped in powdered sugar or jam and accompanied with mulled wine called gløgg. I got addicted to Pebernødder (page 224), tiny crunchy cinnamon cookies that shopkeepers put out in bowls for customers throughout December. That whole month in Denmark is extremely festive, with jolly winter markets and pretty lights strung everywhere.

But even when the holidays are over, the winter fun (and feasting) goes on. For those unfamiliar with the Christian tradition of Lent, it is a period of forty days starting in late February lasting into early April, in which religious people traditionally fast or abstain from treats. That might not sound particularly jolly, but it has led to a lot of pre-Lent indulgence as folks prepared for a season of deprivation. It's why we've got Mardi Gras ("Fat Tuesday") in New Orleans, a day to feast before the fasting began. Similarly, in Scandinavia people spend the period before Lent, in January and February, regularly eating delicious treats specific to this time of year, like cream-filled chocolate-covered buns in Denmark; almond-and-cream-filled buns in Sweden; and cream-and-jam-filled buns in Norway.

Once I discovered and embraced the pleasures of Scandinavian winter, things got infinitely better. In fact, after a friend of mine dared me to jump in the cold water of the Copenhagen harbor, I found the experience so invigorating that I even joined a "plunge club" and swiftly became addicted to early morning dips. Of course, these were always followed by a hot sauna and a stop at one of my favorite bakeries for a buttery tebirkes or a gooey cinnamon knot before heading off to work.

During my fifteen years in Denmark, I came to embrace those winter months. Winter means enjoying the cold nipping at your nose and ears when outside and cuddling up on the couch with a plate of cookies, tea, and a bulky blanket (and perhaps a loved one or two as well) when you're inside. It's about comforting stews, condensation on the kitchen windows, cookie tins, and warm spices. Winter is the dark time, when the landscape recovers from the endless summer and recharges for the following spring. The simpleness of winter (including the scarcity of seasonal produce) is a necessary step in the cycle of the seasons, but I never thought about it like that until I found out how to make the most of it like the Scandinavians do.

GINGER CRISPS WITH BLACK PEPPER AND CANDIED ORANGE PEEL

Brunkager

This is one of the first holiday cookie recipes that I learned how to bake from my Danish mother-in-law. These ginger crisps are made by chilling logs of buttery dough that contain a variety of warming spices and whole almonds. After the logs are refrigerated, the nuts soften enough that you can slice the logs thinly, cutting right through the almonds, with a result that looks nougat-like. They also include orange peel candied in a simple syrup that softens the rind and imparts an appealing chewiness to the crisp cookies.

While these cookies are simple and delicious, plan to make your candied orange peel and chill the dough a few days before you want to bake the cookies. Since the recipe yields four logs of dough, I suggest baking these cookies in batches, wrapping and refrigerating the portion of dough you don't need right away. There is no egg in this dough, so it can be left in the refrigerator for up to two weeks. Slice into a log on demand to have hot ginger crisps available when holiday company drops by or the urge for a freshly baked cookie strikes.

MAKES 60 TO 75 COOKIES

- 1 cup (226 g) unsalted butter
- ⅓ cup (100 g) light corn syrup
- 1¼ cups (250 g) sugar
- 3¾ cups (480 g) all-purpose flour
- ¾ cup (100 g) raw whole almonds (skin on)
- 2 tablespoons coarsely chopped candied orange peel (page 223)
- 1 tablespoon ground cinnamon
- 2 teaspoons ground ginger
- 1 teaspoon ground cloves
- 1 teaspoon ground allspice

→ INGREDIENTS CONTINUED

In a small saucepan, heat the butter over medium heat until just melted, then add the corn syrup and sugar, stirring to combine. Remove from the heat and allow the mixture to cool in the pan to room temperature. (There is no need for the sugar to dissolve completely, as it will do so later.)

In the bowl of a stand mixer, whisk by hand the flour, almonds, candied orange peel, cinnamon, ginger, cloves, allspice, baking soda, pepper, and salt.

Add the cooled butter mixture to the flour mixture. Using the paddle attachment, mix everything until thoroughly combined; it should have a claylike consistency. You may need to get your hands in the mixer bowl at the end to finish the dough. If it isn't quite coming together, add 1 tablespoon water.

Divide the dough into four equal portions. Roll each portion into a log about 8 inches (20 cm) long and 1½ inches (3.5 cm) wide. I don't flour my work surface before doing this, but if you find that the dough is sticking, add just a pinch of flour to your work surface before proceeding. Wrap each portion in parchment paper or plastic wrap and chill for 24 to 48 hours in the refrigerator. This long chilling time allows the nuts to soften enough for you to slice right through them.

CONTINUED

GINGER CRISPS WITH BLACK PEPPER AND CANDIED ORANGE PEEL, CONTINUED

2 teaspoons baking soda

½ teaspoon freshly ground black pepper (see Note)

½ teaspoon kosher salt

When ready to bake, line two 13 by 18-inch (33 by 46 cm) baking trays with parchment paper. Arrange two racks in the upper and lower thirds of the oven and preheat the oven to 325°F (165°C).

Using a very sharp chef's knife, slice each log into ⅛-inch-thick (3 mm) slices and place them ½ inch (1 cm) apart on the prepared baking trays. You should have about twenty cookies per tray. If your knife isn't sharp enough, you may run into difficulty slicing through the whole almonds, which will make the dough crumble. The cookies should be as thin as possible without falling apart as you cut them. Aim for consistency of thickness. If some are thick and others are thin, they will bake at different times, and the thin ones will get crispy (and could burn) while the thick ones will stay undercooked. If the dough gets too soft to cut to a consistent thinness, pop it back in the refrigerator for 30 minutes more or so. Any dough scraps can be gathered into a log, chilled, and then sliced as well.

Bake for 5 to 6 minutes, then rotate the baking trays from top to bottom and front to back and bake for an additional 4 minutes, or until golden brown and slightly darker at the edges. The cookies should be fairly firm to the touch, although they will continue crisping after you take them out of the oven. Transfer the cookies to a rack to cool and continue to bake the rest of the dough in batches.

After the cookies have cooled completely, store them in a cookie tin or other airtight container, where they should stay crisp and delicious for 1 to 2 weeks. If they soften a bit after having been stored, bake them for 2 to 3 minutes in a preheated 350°F (175°C) to recrisp them.

NOTE First grind the pepper into a small bowl. This makes it easier to scoop out the precise amount needed.

CANDIED ORANGE PEEL

The orange peel isn't "candied" in the sense of being dried out. Instead, orange peel slices get blanched, boiled in a simple syrup, and then stored in a jar with the syrup, to be used as desired. As long as the peel stays submerged in the simple syrup, it will stay fresh for at least a month in the refrigerator. Use organic produce whenever possible, especially in preparations like this where the peel will be eaten.

This candied orange peel is a wonderful ingredient to have on hand in the kitchen. Chopped, it's great tossed with fresh fruit on pancakes or as a porridge topping. It can also serve as the garnish for a festive holiday cocktail: think something with aquavit! I've even pureed this candied orange peel to add to delicious salad dressings and marinades. At Kantine, we brush this orange simple syrup over our St. Lucia Day Saffron Buns (page 243), so if you have some in the refrigerator, there's no need to make more. MAKES 1½ CUPS (185 G)

3 organic oranges

1½ cups (300 g) sugar

1½ cups (360 g) water

Using a paring knife, cut the peel off of each orange, trying not to take too much of the white pith off with the peel. Slice the peel into ¼-inch-wide (6 mm) strips. Place them in a saucepan and cover them with water. Bring the water to a boil and blanch the peels for 10 minutes. Drain the water, rinse the peels, and cover again with water. Bring to a boil and blanch for 10 minutes more. This process removes the bitterness from the peel. Remove the slices of orange peel with a slotted spoon, set them aside, and discard the water.

In the same saucepan, combine the sugar and the water. Over medium-high heat, bring the liquid to a boil, stirring to dissolve the sugar. Add the orange peel and return the mixture to a boil. Turn off the heat and let the mixture cool to room temperature in the pan. Transfer the orange peel, with the simple syrup, to a jar or other airtight container until ready to use. Store in the refrigerator for up to 1 month.

CINNAMON BUTTONS
Pebernødder

In Denmark, all through the month of December, these tiny, crisp, round cinnamon cookies are likely to be found in bowls by the register at any shop. It's almost too easy to keep popping them into your mouth, completely losing track of how many you've had by the time you finish buying presents off your list. This was another cookie that my Danish mother-in-law taught me how to bake, but I always made it by her side and never bothered writing down the recipe. After she passed away, I was relieved to find that my sister-in-law had copied it down and could share it with me. MAKES 50 TO 60 BITE-SIZE COOKIES

½ cup plus 1 tablespoon (127 g) unsalted butter, at room temperature

⅔ cup (125 g) sugar

1 egg

2¼ cups (288 g) all-purpose flour, plus more for dusting

1 teaspoon baking soda

½ teaspoon ground ginger

½ teaspoon ground cinnamon

½ teaspoon freshly ground decorticated cardamom (see page 21)

Pinch of ground white pepper

¼ teaspoon kosher salt

In the bowl of a stand mixer fitted with the paddle attachment, beat the butter and sugar until creamy and well combined, pausing halfway through to scrape the sides and bottom of the bowl with a rubber spatula. Add the egg, flour, baking soda, ginger, cinnamon, cardamom, white pepper, and salt and mix on low speed until everything is just incorporated, finishing the dough by hand if needed.

Chill the dough, covered, for at least 1 hour in the refrigerator.

Line two 13 by 18-inch (33 by 46 cm) baking trays with parchment paper. Arrange two racks in the upper and lower thirds of the oven and preheat the oven to 400°F (200°C).

Divide the dough into four equal portions. Lightly dust a work surface with flour, then roll each portion into a thin log about ½ inch (1 cm) in diameter. Using a chef's knife, cut the logs at ½-inch (1 cm) intervals and roll each slice into a ball.

Place the balls on the prepared baking trays, spaced about ½ inch (1 cm) apart.

Bake for 7 to 9 minutes, rotating the baking trays halfway through from top to bottom and front to back. They will turn a slightly darker brown while baking and fill your kitchen with a delicious aroma. Transfer the cookies to a rack to cool completely. Store the cookies in an airtight container, where they will stay fresh for up to 4 days.

VANILLA WREATH COOKIES

Vaniljekranse

As kids in the Midwest, my siblings and I never got an allowance. To get spending money, we had to earn it. As a teen, I served coffee and doughnuts at my father's Mister Donut franchise. One December, I got the idea to bake and sell Danish wreath cookies for extra cash. This was before I had even been to Scandinavia or seen examples of these made from scratch! I literally baked at home for days, and the results looked nothing like the perfectly shaped ring cookies in the blue tin that had served as my inspiration. However, once I brought the cookies into work to sell, all of our regulars bought them and I sold out in just a few hours, permanently cementing my belief that homemade is best!

Now that I know what I'm doing—and have come to understand the utility of a pastry bag—I can create cookies that look much closer to my favorites from the royal blue tin. The vanilla butter dough comes together quickly, and then it's just a matter of squeezing it into a circular shape from a piping bag with a star-shaped tip for those fluted edges (see page 31).

MAKES 24 COOKIES

- 1 cup (226 g) unsalted butter, at room temperature
- ¾ cup (175 g) sugar
- 1 egg
- 1 teaspoon vanilla extract
- 2 cups (256 g) all-purpose flour
- ¾ cup (80 g) almond flour
- 1 teaspoon kosher salt

In the bowl of a stand mixer fitted with the paddle attachment or in a large bowl with a handheld mixer, beat the butter and sugar on medium until soft and creamy, pausing halfway through to scrape the sides and bottom of the bowl with a rubber spatula, about 3 minutes. Add the egg and vanilla and mix again to incorporate.

In a medium bowl, whisk together the all-purpose flour, almond flour, and salt. Add the flour mixture to the butter mixture and beat on low until just combined.

Line two 13 by 18-inch (33 by 46 cm) baking trays with parchment paper. Arrange two racks in the upper and lower thirds of the oven and preheat the oven to 325°F (165°C).

Draw three neat rows of four circles each onto each piece of parchment paper, where you will pipe twelve cookies per tray. I recommend tracing quarters to form the inside of each wreath. Space them 3 inches (7.5 cm) apart on the parchment paper, so that you have ample space to "draw" with your piping bag full of dough. The diameter of each cookie should be 2 inches (5 cm). Then, flip the paper over, so that the inky side faces down (but you can still see the markings through it).

"Glue" these sheets of parchment paper to the baking trays by using a pinch of dough to stick down each corner. This will anchor them in place while you pipe cookies.

CONTINUED

Attach a medium star-shaped tip to a pastry bag and then fill it with the cookie dough, using a rubber spatula to scoop the batter from the mixing bowl into the bag. Aim to get as much volume as possible down near the tip rather than smeared up top. To make this process easier, prop the bag in a canister of some sort, like a French press coffee pot, a vase, or an empty quart container. Turn the bag's top edge down around the top of the empty container. This lets you use both hands to fill it rather than having to awkwardly hold it in one hand while filling it with the other.

Unfold the top of the piping bag and remove it from the container. Using your nondominant hand, twist the top of the piping bag to remove air and start to push the dough toward the tip. Keep your dominant hand right above the tip as you do this. Hold the tip low over the cookie sheet as you squeeze the bag, making a wreath shape around each predrawn circle. Once the wreath is complete, lower the tip, pressing it against the piped dough to cut it off. If you want to be fussy, you can moisten a fingertip and smooth out the seam and any other imperfections, but baking is likely to erase whatever "mistakes" you may have made in piping. Also, once people taste these cookies, it's unlikely you will hear any criticism! Repeat with the remaining dough.

Bake for 16 to 18 minutes, rotating the baking trays halfway through from top to bottom and front to back, until the edges are lightly golden. Let the cookies cool on the trays for a few minutes before transferring them to a rack to cool completely. Store the cookies in a tin or other airtight container, where they will stay fresh for up to 5 days.

HAZELNUT CARDAMOM MATCHSTICKS

Hazelnuts are commonly eaten in Scandinavia around the holidays, which gave me the idea to create this riff on Finnish Almond Matchsticks (page 43). The inclusion of hazelnuts and crunchy, glittering cardamom sugar sprinkled on top make these bite-size cookies festive enough to go in any holiday cookie tin. MAKES 16 COOKIES

- ⅓ cup (50 g) whole hazelnuts
- 1 cup (226 g) cold unsalted butter, cut into tablespoon-size pieces
- 2 cups (256 g) all-purpose flour
- 1⅓ cups (266 g) granulated sugar
- ½ teaspoon kosher salt
- 1 teaspoon freshly ground decorticated cardamom (see page 21)
- 1 teaspoon vanilla extract
- 1 egg
- 2 tablespoons cardamom sugar (see page 77)

In a food processor, pulse the hazelnuts to a coarse sand, being careful not to turn them into nut butter. (If your food processor has a 3-cup capacity or less, transfer the hazelnuts to the bowl of a stand mixer fitted with the paddle attachment. Otherwise, proceed with making the dough in the food processor.) Add the butter, flour, granulated sugar, salt, and cardamom. Process or mix until the dough starts to clump, then add the vanilla. Process or mix until it forms a ball.

Wrap the dough in parchment paper or plastic wrap and refrigerate it for at least 30 minutes. Because this dough doesn't contain eggs, it can be refrigerated safely at this point for up to 1 week to bake on a later day.

When you are ready to bake the cookies, line two 13 by 18-inch (33 by 46 cm) baking trays with parchment paper. Arrange two racks in the upper and lower thirds of the oven and preheat the oven to 350°F (175°C).

After removing the dough from the refrigerator, you may need to let it temper on the counter until it's warm enough to manipulate. Don't be afraid to work it a bit. Divide the dough into four equal portions. Roll each portion into a 16-inch-long (40 cm) log about ½ inch (1 cm) in diameter. I don't flour my counter before doing this, but if you find that it is sticking, add a pinch of flour to your work surface. With a chef's knife, cut the logs into 2-inch-wide (5 cm) pieces (eight cookies per log), trying to keep the cut round edges blunt. Transfer the matchstick cookies to the prepared baking trays, spacing them about 1 inch (2.5 cm) apart.

In a small bowl, whisk the egg with a fork. Using a pastry brush, lightly brush the top of each cookie with the egg wash and then sprinkle with the cardamom sugar.

Bake for 12 to 14 minutes, rotating the baking trays halfway through from top to bottom and front to back, until golden at the edges. They will continue to crisp up as they cool, but if you like them on the crispier side, bake them slightly longer, otherwise they will still stay a bit soft. Transfer the cookies to a rack to cool before enjoying. Store them in an airtight container, where they will stay fresh for up to 1 week.

HONEY HEARTS

Honninghjerter

The first time I saw these hearts at the bakery, I found them very peculiar. Not because of their sheer size (I see nothing wrong with that!), but because they were garnished with glossy pieces of paper that seemed to be cut out of a 1950s-themed Christmas card or storybook. Some were of Santa with his big white beard and red hat, others were of cherub-faced children sledding in the snow or holding ornately packaged presents. I was so intrigued that I bought one to figure out exactly what this was, only to find that the paper was inedible (yes, I tried) and the cookie under the chocolate shell was as chewy as a soft oatmeal cookie but more substantial and flavored with all the best warm spices.

Lots of recipes for these hearts will advise you to make the dough at least a month in advance of baking, but I'm not that patient, so I devised my own recipe that can be baked right away if the craving calls, still producing the right texture and taste. The cookies are covered with tempered chocolate and decorated with royal icing. They are so pretty that some Danes even string them up and hang them on their Christmas tree as ornaments! **MAKES 8 TO 10 HEARTS, DEPENDING ON THE SIZE OF YOUR COOKIE CUTTER**

¾ cup plus 1 tablespoon (250 g) honey

½ cup (100 g) sugar

⅓ cup (75 g) unsalted butter

4 cups (512 g) all-purpose flour, plus more for dusting

2 teaspoons baking powder

1½ teaspoons ground cinnamon

½ teaspoon freshly ground decorticated cardamom (see page 21)

¼ teaspoon ground cloves

¼ teaspoon kosher salt

1 egg

To finish

5 ounces (141 g) 63% (or higher) bittersweet chocolate, broken or chopped into pieces (see Note, page 60)

In a small saucepan, whisk the honey, sugar, and butter over medium heat until melted. Transfer the mixture to the bowl of a stand mixer and allow to cool for 10 minutes.

In a large bowl, combine the flour, baking powder, cinnamon, cardamom, cloves, and salt.

By hand, whisk the egg into the honey mixture. Add the flour mixture to the honey mixture and, using the dough hook attachment, mix on medium speed until uniform in color, about 3 minutes. The dough will be slightly sticky, so wrap it in plastic wrap and chill for 30 minutes in the refrigerator before using. It can also be safely refrigerated for up to 2 weeks.

When you are ready to bake the cookies, line two 13 by 18-inch (33 by 46 cm) baking trays with parchment paper. Arrange two racks in the upper and lower thirds of the oven and preheat the oven to 350°F (175°C).

Lightly dust a work surface with flour, then roll out the dough to ½-inch (1 cm) thickness. (These cookies are meant to be thick, just in case you were in doubt.) Cut the dough into hearts using cutters—my favorite is a 5-inch (13 cm) heart—and transfer to the prepared baking trays, spacing them 1 inch (2.5 cm) apart. Feel free to reroll your scraps to make more cookies.

CONTINUED

Bake for 20 to 25 minutes, rotating the baking trays halfway through from top to bottom and front to back, until light brown and firm to the touch—the baking time will depend a bit on the size of your hearts. Transfer the hearts to a rack to cool.

When completely cool, transfer the cookies to an airtight container and cover them with a piece of parchment paper followed by a damp kitchen towel. Seal the container and refrigerate for a minimum of 1 day or up to 4 days. Putting the hearts in the refrigerator is not obligatory but strongly suggested as it makes the hearts magically and wonderfully chewy.

TO FINISH, TEMPER THE CHOCOLATE

Tempering chocolate is a process of melting chocolate slowly that gives it a smooth and glossy finish and allows it to set well on baked goods. Place three-quarters of the chocolate in a medium heat-resistant bowl. Fill a saucepan with about 1 inch of water and bring to a low simmer. Place the bowl over (but not touching) the simmering water. Stir the chocolate occasionally until almost entirely melted. Remove the bowl from the saucepan (keep the heat on) and stir to melt remaining bits. Add the rest of the chopped chocolate to the melted chocolate and stir to combine. Place the bowl back over the simmering water and heat, stirring often, until almost entirely melted. Be sure not to let the chocolate get warmer than 88°F (31°C). Dip the fronts of the hearts in the chocolate and allow them to dry on a rack. As they dry, make the icing from Marzipan Wreath Tower (page 239) and make a parchment paper piping bag (see page 240). Decorate the chocolate-covered hearts however you like. The cookies can be served right away or stored in an airtight container for up to 4 days.

GINGERBREAD CUTOUT COOKIES

Pepparkakor

No Scandinavian holiday cookie chapter would be complete without a gingerbread cookie. What we call gingerbread the Swedes call pepparkakor, or "pepper cookies." Black pepper adds a sharp, piney note to the other spices in this Swedish holiday favorite, which are usually cut into heart, flower, or star shapes. My Swedish friend Line Shou provided the inspiration for this recipe, and she prefers to make the dough at least a week in advance of baking because she swears it makes the spices come alive.

The addition of so much flour results in an unusually hard and crunchy cookie, which means that the dough can be used as the walls and roof of a gingerbread house as well as for making ornaments. However, it's also delicious, while the gingerbread houses that you buy in kits are often not. Making edible decorations is a great green initiative that minimizes the need for storage after the holidays.

Dip the edges of your cookie cutter in a bowl of flour to make it easier to cut the cookies out and transfer them to baking trays. Unlike American gingerbread cutout cookies, these don't get decorated with icing. One bite and I think you'll agree that no garnish is needed. **MAKES 30 TO 60 COOKIES, DEPENDING ON THE SIZE OF YOUR COOKIE CUTTER**

- ⅔ cup (150 g) unsalted butter, at room temperature
- 2 cups (400 g) sugar
- ¾ cup (85 g) water
- ½ cup (140 g) molasses
- ⅓ cup (110 g) light corn syrup
- 3 cups (790 g) all-purpose flour, plus more for dusting
- 1 tablespoon baking soda
- 1 tablespoon ground cinnamon
- 1 tablespoon ground cloves
- 1 tablespoon ground ginger
- 4 or 5 grinds of black pepper
- ½ teaspoon kosher salt

In the bowl of a stand mixer fitted with the paddle attachment, beat the butter and sugar on medium until soft and creamy, pausing halfway through to scrape the sides and bottom of the bowl with a rubber spatula, about 3 minutes. Add the water, molasses, and corn syrup and mix until well combined.

In a large bowl, whisk the flour, baking soda, cinnamon, cloves, ginger, pepper, and salt. Add the flour mixture to the butter mixture and mix on low until it forms a shaggy dough, 2 to 3 minutes. You may want to drape a kitchen towel around the mouth of the mixer bowl at first in order to keep the flour contained.

Lightly dust a work surface with flour. Turn out the dough onto your work surface and knead it well. Because this is a relatively dry dough with a lot of flour, you will definitely need (no pun intended) to work it with your hands for the ball to come together. Wrap the dough in parchment paper or plastic wrap and chill it for 5 to 7 days in the refrigerator for best results. Chilling this buttery dough locks in the flavor of all of those comforting holiday spices.

CONTINUED

When you are ready to bake the cookies, line two 13 by 18-inch (33 by 46 cm) baking trays with parchment paper. Arrange two racks in the upper and lower thirds of the oven and preheat the oven to 350°F (175°C).

Remove your dough from the refrigerator (you may need to let the chilled dough temper for 5 minutes until it softens enough to be pliable) and divide it into four portions. Lightly dust a work surface with flour and, working one piece at a time, roll each portion out to approximately ⅛-inch (3 mm) thickness. Cut it into shapes with a cookie cutter or create the walls and roof of a gingerbread house, drawing them out first on paper. Scraps can be combined, chilled, and rerolled to cut into more cookies. The internet has a wealth of templates and patterns for gingerbread houses, for which this dough would work perfectly. Place the cookies on the prepared baking trays, 1 inch (2.5 cm) apart.

Bake for 10 to 15 minutes, then rotate each tray from top to bottom and front to back and bake for 5 to 7 minutes more, until set and lightly browned at the edges. Let the cookies cool slightly before transferring them to a rack to cool completely. Store the cookies in an airtight container, where they will stay fresh for 1 to 2 weeks. They should also stay crisp enough to hold their shape when used as the walls and roof of a gingerbread house, staying tasty longer than you might imagine!

APPLE DUMPLINGS WITH BUTTERMILK AND LEMON ZEST

Æbleskiver

New to Denmark, I threw myself into making a slew of traditional Danish dishes. To this day, one of my favorites remains æbleskiver, or Danish "apple dumplings." These holiday treats are made by rotating balls of eggy batter in a special pan using the tip of a skewer. Although the name suggests otherwise, they don't require an apple-filled center, so I'll leave the decision of with or without up to you. For the most part, these are only eaten around the holidays, most often at gatherings held in the afternoon, served with strawberry jam and powdered sugar alongside mulled wine or coffee. Most Danes purchase frozen æbleskiver from the supermarket, but homemade ones are in a league of their own: pillowy and soft on the inside with crisp and buttery contoured edges.

Making them does require an æbleskiver pan (see page 33), which looks similar to an egg-poaching pan, its indentations creating the golf ball shape. You fill these divots with batter, then use a skewer (or, traditionally, a knitting needle!) to nudge the cooked part up and continue drizzling more batter into each well, gradually rotating and adding more batter until you've got perfect buttery balls. The following is a riff on my mother-in-law's recipe for apple dumplings, which feature chunks of apple at the center of each ball. **MAKES ABOUT 24 DUMPLINGS**

½ cup (113 g) unsalted butter

4 eggs, separated

¼ cup (42 g) granulated sugar

1½ teaspoons freshly ground decorticated cardamom (see page 21)

Zest of 1 lemon

1¾ cups (394 g) buttermilk

1½ cups (192 g) all-purpose flour

2 teaspoons baking powder

Pinch of kosher salt

1 tart apple, peeled, cored, and chopped into ½-inch (1 cm) pieces (optional)

½ cup (65 g) powdered sugar

½ cup (130 g) strawberry or raspberry jam

In a small saucepan, melt the butter over low heat. Set aside to cool in the pan.

In a medium bowl, whisk the egg yolks, granulated sugar, cardamom, and lemon zest until light in color. Add the buttermilk and whisk again.

In a medium bowl, whisk the flour and baking powder, then add it to the egg yolk mixture and stir to combine. Stir in ⅓ cup (75 g) of the cooled melted butter, reserving the rest to use to butter the æbleskiver pan.

In the bowl of a stand mixer fitted with the whisk attachment, whisk the egg whites with the salt until soft peaks form, 3 to 4 minutes, then gently fold them into the egg yolk mixture. Allow the batter to rest for about 30 minutes at room temperature before cooking.

Place a baking tray or oven-safe platter in the oven to hold the finished æbleskiver and keep them warm as you make them in batches, then preheat the oven to 200°F (95°C).

To make the æbleskiver, heat the æbleskiver pan over medium heat. With a pastry brush, add a little of the melted butter to

each indentation in the pan. Once the butter is frothy, add enough batter to fill each indentation to the rim. Once the batter has begun to brown and you can see bubbles forming around the edges, about 2 minutes, use a skewer (they usually come with these pans) or toothpick to nudge the dough up on one side of the indentation. Slip a chunk of apple (if using) into the center of the ball and pour more batter into the pan, filling in the area where you lifted and moved the cooked batter aside. Keep using your skewer to turn the balls, gradually filling them in with a little more batter and adding a bit of melted butter as they cook to get an even golden color. The æbleskiver usually take 5 to 7 minutes total to cook, but possibly a bit longer when you're first getting the hang of this. Just keep the heat low and take your time. You can make a small slit, if necessary, to be entirely sure the centers aren't wet. Once they are set and uniformly browned, remove them from the pan and place them in the oven while you cook the remaining batter.

Serve the æbleskiver warm, accompanied by the powdered sugar and jam, plus a mug of hot mulled wine if you want the full Danish holiday experience.

MARZIPAN WREATH TOWER

Kransekake

Talk about a centerpiece that wows: this is the one that folks remember! Like the French croquembouche, it stands taller than anything else on the table. In Norway and Denmark, it's served when there's a celebration underway, usually at confirmations, baptisms, and always on New Year's Eve, where the accompanying drink of choice is champagne. Sometimes kransekake is made in small logs or balls instead of rings, so if you're in the mood to give this recipe a try but don't want to fuss with the special ring molds used to make the tower, you can definitely fashion it however you like. While this dessert doesn't involve much active baking time, it does take three days to make from start to finish, because you must first refrigerate the dough overnight and then refrigerate the baked rings overnight as well. But it's worth the wait. As in the case of the Honey Hearts (page 230), refrigeration turns this confection soft and chewy, two things that make it irresistible. MAKES ONE 8-INCH-TALL (20 CM) TOWER

2½ cups (260 g) almond flour

3 cups (360 g) powdered sugar

½ teaspoon kosher salt

¼ teaspoon almond extract

2 egg whites

Unsalted butter, at room temperature, for the molds

¼ cup (30 g) breadcrumbs, for the molds

All-purpose flour for dusting

Royal icing

2 cups (280 g) powdered sugar

2 egg whites

In the bowl of a stand mixer fitted with the paddle attachment, mix the almond flour, powdered sugar, and salt on low for less than 1 minute. Add the almond extract and egg whites and mix until a stiff dough forms. Wrap the dough tightly in plastic wrap and chill in the refrigerator overnight.

When you're ready to bake the kransekake, preheat the oven to 300°F (150°C). Brush a set of six kransekake molds with butter and sprinkle with the breadcrumbs. (The breadcrumbs won't be noticeable in the final tower, but they help keep the baked rings from sticking.) Very lightly dust a work surface with flour and, working in batches, roll the dough out into long ropes that are slightly thicker than pencils. Transfer each rope to the molds, cutting them to size. Place the molds on a baking tray and bake for about 30 minutes, until puffed and lightly golden brown on the underside. (If you can't fit all your molds in the oven at the same time, bake them in batches.)

Transfer the molds to a rack and cool completely. Carefully remove the rings from molds. Place the rings in an airtight container, adding a piece of parchment paper between each ring to prevent sticking, and refrigerate overnight or for up to 3 days before assembling.

CONTINUED

MAKE THE ICING

In the bowl of a stand mixer fitted with the whisk attachment, combine the powdered sugar and egg whites and mix on medium until thick, pausing halfway through to scrape the sides and bottom of the bowl with a rubber spatula, about 6 minutes.

Assemble the kransekake on a clean work surface. Sort the rings in order of size. Fill a small piping bag or a piping bag fashioned out of parchment paper with the icing. Pipe a thin stream of icing onto the largest ring in a loopy, ornate fashion (see photograph, opposite), rotating the ring as you work. The icing acts both as a decoration and a glue for the next ring. Place the next largest ring directly on top and continue to pipe as you work through the rings in decreasing size. Allow the icing to set before transferring to a platter and serving.

PAPER PIPING BAGS

Cut a piece of parchment paper into a triangle about 12 by 12 by 18 inches (30.5 by 30.5 by 46 cm). With the longest side facing away from you, turn one "wing" up toward the point closest to you, creating a cone with a flap hanging off one side. While holding the first wing in place, wrap the second wing around the cone. Inch the tips of each flap against each other until the cone tip has completely closed. Fold the edge of the cone to secure flap tips in place and put the piping bag in a cup to facilitate filling it. Fold the top closed once filled and snip just the tip of the bag off when ready to start piping.

ST. LUCIA DAY SAFFRON BUNS

Lussekatter

Tinted a bright yellow from saffron, these sweet-and-tender buns are served in Sweden around December 13, or St. Lucia Day, a winter solstice celebration. Legend has it that the martyred St. Lucia once appeared in Sweden during the darkest part of the year, lighting the way with her crown of candles. Every year on this cold December morning, the eldest daughter in any Swedish household is supposed to bring breakfast in bed to her parents while wearing a white gown and a crown made of candles. It's a Swedish tradition from before the Lutheran reform, blending Old Norse with Catholicism. But many Swedes still uphold it faithfully (although crowns of electrically lit candles now often replace the flammable version) and welcome the chance to bake and partake in saffron lussekatter: buns garnished with an orange-scented glaze and raisins. **MAKES 18 BUNS**

Tangzhong

3 tablespoons all-purpose flour

½ cup (120 g) whole milk

Dough

½ cup (113 g) unsalted butter, cut into 1-inch (2.5 cm) pieces at room temperature, plus more for greasing

1½ cups (360 g) whole milk

1 heaping teaspoon saffron threads

4½ cups (576 g) all-purpose flour, plus more for dusting

2½ teaspoons kosher salt

2 eggs

1 tablespoon active dry yeast

⅓ cup (66 g) sugar

36 raisins

Orange simple syrup glaze

2 tablespoons water

2 tablespoons sugar

Zest of ½ orange

MAKE THE TANGZHONG

In a small saucepan, whisk the flour and milk so there are no lumps. Cook over medium heat, whisking constantly, until the mixture becomes elastic with the consistency of thick glue, about 1 minute. Transfer the mixture to the bowl of a stand mixer and let it cool completely, about 10 minutes.

MAKE THE DOUGH

Butter a medium bowl and line two 13 by 18-inch (33 by 46 cm) baking trays with parchment paper.

In a small saucepan, combine the milk and saffron threads and bring to a simmer over medium-high heat. Remove the pot from the heat as soon as bubbles form at the edge of the pan. Allow the saffron to steep for about 15 minutes, until the milk cools. The milk should turn yellow and feel lukewarm to the touch when you add it to the bowl of the stand mixer. Be careful to scrape the edges of the pan to make sure no saffron is left behind.

To the bowl of the stand mixer, add the flour, salt, 1 of the eggs, and the yeast. With the paddle attachment, mix on medium until all the ingredients are combined, pausing to scrape the sides and bottom of the bowl with a rubber spatula, about 2 minutes. Increase the speed to medium and mix for 4 minutes more. Decrease the speed to low and sprinkle in the sugar, 1 tablespoon at a time. Gradually add the butter, one or two pieces at a time, waiting between each addition for them to be incorporated into the dough, then mix for 4 minutes more. The butter should be completely absorbed into a glossy dough that looks more elastic than before.

Transfer the dough to the prepared bowl. Cover it with a kitchen towel or plastic wrap and chill for least 1 hour or overnight (up to 12 hours) in the refrigerator.

Lightly dust a work surface with flour. Divide the dough into eighteen portions of approximately 80 g each. For precision, weigh each portion with a digital scale. (I recommend forming three equal-size logs. Then portion each log into six pieces using your bench scraper and scale.) Clean any residual dough off of the work surface with a bench scraper, then lightly dust again with flour.

To shape the buns, form each portion into a ball by rolling it under your palm until it feels fairly round and smooth. You don't need it to be perfectly round. Roll a ball of dough into a snake, 12 to 14 inches (30 to 35 cm) long. Curl one end of the snake into a coil, stopping at the midpoint. Curl the other end into a coil in the opposite direction, stopping at the midpoint where it meets the first coil; the bun should look like a figure eight. Place the bun on one of the prepared baking trays and repeat with the remaining dough balls. You should have nine buns per tray, spaced 2 inches (5 cm) apart.

PROOF THE BUNS

Cover the baking trays with plastic wrap or a kitchen towel and place them in a warm, draft-free spot on the countertop for 30 minutes to 1 hour. The buns are done proofing when an indentation made in the dough with your fingertip is slow to fill in. Alternatively, see page 36 for the oven-proofing method.

When the buns are sufficiently proofed, preheat the oven to 350°F (175°C).

In a small bowl, whisk the egg with a fork. Using a pastry brush, lightly brush the entire surface of each bun with the egg wash. Place 1 raisin in the center of each coil, for a total of 2 raisins per bun.

Bake for 20 to 25 minutes, rotating the baking trays halfway through from top to bottom and front to back, until the buns are a light golden brown. Transfer the buns to a rack to cool until you can handle them comfortably before brushing with the simple syrup.

MAKE THE SIMPLE SYRUP

In a small pot, combine the water and sugar over medium-high heat, stirring until the sugar is dissolved. Remove the pot from the heat and let it cool completely. Stir in the zest.

With a pastry brush, brush the surface of each bun with the syrup.

St. Lucia saffron buns are best enjoyed warm on the day they are baked. They can be toasted and smothered in cold butter if enjoying a day or two later.

ACKNOWLEDGMENTS

Thank you/Tak/Tack/Takk!

My loving family, especially my partner, Joachim, and our not-so-small kids. I am so lucky to have your constant support and understanding, and I adore your insatiable willingness to forever be my taste testers.

Malena Watrous, this book's cowriter. You dove right into the subject of Scandinavian baking and wove all the pieces and parts that were swirling around in my head together so beautifully. Thank you for being so fun, funny, and dedicated.

Jennifer Aaronson, this book's stylist and my kitchen sister. We can chalk this one up as another adventure together. Your positive energy and creativity, which you maintain even when the going gets tough, are both admirable and contagious.

Anders Schønnemann, this book's photographer. You brought this book to life with color and skill. Thank you for hosting us in your studio in Copenhagen—we almost moved in!

Katherine Cowles, my agent. You push me, teach me, and stand by my side.

The entire staff of Kantine, both past and present. I appreciate you all for your commitment to preserving a workplace that is positive, all-inclusive, and utterly delicious.

Kantine regulars. So much gratitude for gathering at our place and continuing to love us as we grow, morph, and, simultaneously, remain the same.

The whole team at Ten Speed Press: Dervla Kelly, Terry Deal, Lizzie Allen, Michelle Gale, Serena Sigona, Kathy Brock, Ivy McFadden, Barbara Mortenson, Andrea Portanova, and Erica Gelbard. Thank you for allowing me to share recipes from my kitchen binder. A special thanks to Aaron Wehner, whose encouragement and support made this book possible.

Mikkel Svane, my dear friend. We've eaten many, many meals together, and some of my best have been the ones I've shared with you. Thank you for your faith as well as your glorious appetite.

Friends who have offered recipes, insight, inspiration, and support during the creation of this book: Paula Holm, Line Schou, Kenneth Højgaard, Tori Richie, Hannah Jacobson, Bruce Cole, Bill Roberts, Tonje Vetletseter, Dorte Brandenhoff, and the "K" Club.

Lucy and Charlie, our test kitchen dogs. You never let things get too serious.

INDEX

Note: *Italicized* pages refer to photos.

Photograph: Stine Christiansen

ABOUT THE AUTHOR

NICHOLE ACCETTOLA is a graduate of the Culinary Institute of America and an American chef who worked in fine dining in Boston before moving to Denmark for fifteen years. In 2015, Nichole and her family moved to sunny California, and she started making Danish rye bread, smørrebrød, and porridges to sell at San Francisco's farmers' markets. The success of that venture inspired Nichole to open a casual, daytime brick and mortar. Seven years later, Kantine (kantinesf.com) is known as the place to go for irresistible Scandinavian foods, including wholesome breads, open-faced sandwiches, pastries, cookies, and cakes. Aside from running Kantine, Nichole has advised the Alice Waters Institute, plays tennis, and her dream of staying at Julia Child's summer cottage in Provence recently came true.

Malena Watrous is the coauthor of the cookbook *My Mexico City Kitchen*, with Gabriela Camara, and the author of the novel *If You Follow Me*. She has contributed reviews and articles to *The New York Times* and the *San Francisco Chronicle*, *Allure*, *Real Simple*, *Condé Nast Traveler*, and other publications.

Published in the United States by Ten Speed Press, an imprint of Random House, a division of Penguin Random House LLC, New York.
TenSpeed.com
RandomHouseBooks.com

Ten Speed Press and the Ten Speed Press colophon are registered trademarks of Penguin Random House LLC.

Interior typefaces: Letters From Sweden's Lab Grotesque and Ivar

Cover typeface: Rasmus Andersson's Inter

Library of Congress Cataloging-in-Publication Data is on file with the publisher.

Hardcover ISBN: 978-1-9848-6194-8
eBook ISBN: 978-1-9848-6195-5

Printed in China

Editor: Dervla Kelly
Principal photographer: Anders Schønnemann
Additional photographers: Alanna Hale (page 10) and Stine Christiansen (page 254)
Production editor: Terry Deal
Designer: Lizzie Allen
Production designers: Mari Gill and Faith Hague
Production manager: Serena Sigona
Prepress color manager: Neil Spitkovsky
Food stylist: Jennifer Aaronson
Props: KH Würtz
Copyeditor: Michelle Gale
Proofreaders: Kathy Brock and Ivy McFadden
Indexer: Barbara Mortenson
Publicist: Erica Gelbard
Marketer: Andrea Portanova

10 9 8 7 6 5 4 3 2 1

First Edition